The 5 Pillars of Amazon Wholesale

Corey Ganim

Copyright © 2024 Corey Ganim

All Rights Reserved

Contents

From College Grad to Amazon Success: My Journey 1

What to Expect in This Book 5
What You WILL Find in This Book 5
What You WON'T Find in This book 7
The Structure of This Book 8

Getting to Grips with Wholesale 9
What Is Amazon Wholesale? 9
Why Amazon? 9
Risks vs. Benefits 10
The Biggest Sellers in Wholesale 12
Approaches to Wholesale 13
The Importance of Choosing a Niche 17
Necessary Tools: A Comprehensive List 19
Setting Up Your Business Structure 22

Core Concepts and Mindset 25
The Compounding Effect of Wholesale 25
Setting Expectations: The Mindset for Success in Amazon Wholesale 28
Capital Requirements 30
Expected Margins 32
Building Relationships in the Business 34

Pillar #1 Finding Suppliers 37
Comparing Brands, Distributors and Wholesalers 37
Choosing Brands to Sell: A Checklist 37
Choosing Distributors to Work With: A Checklist 39
Finding Brand-Direct Leads with SmartScout 41
Verifying Brand Criteria 43
Finding Brand-Direct Leads Using Amazon's Website 44
Finding Brand-Direct Leads by Spying on Other Sellers 46
Finding Brand-Direct Leads Using Google 48
Finding Brand-Direct Leads Using SpyFu 50
Finding Distributors by Spotting Local Opportunities 51

Finding Leads Through Trade Show Exhibitor Lists 53
Finding Leads by Attending Trade Shows 55
Finding and Utilizing Supplier Contact Information 58
Compiling Supplier Contact Information 60
Building Great Relationships with Suppliers 62

Pillar #2 Contacting Suppliers 65
Dos and Don'ts of Contacting Suppliers 65
Following Up Appropriately 67
Strategies for Contacting Suppliers: Combo Hits 69
Strategies for Contacting Suppliers: Triple Dial 71
Positioning Yourself Effectively When Contacting Suppliers 73
Reaching Decision-Makers 75
Utilizing LinkedIn to Contact Suppliers 77
Email Outreach: Sample Templates 78

Pillar #3 Sourcing Products 81
Opening Supplier Accounts and Accessing Pricing 81
Using UPC Scanners to Simplify Sourcing 83
Reverse Sourcing 85
SmartScout Reverse Sourcing 87
Unlocking More Inventory with Special Orders 89
How to Ask for a Discount 91
Using a Simple Purchasing Criterion 93
Determining Purchase Quantities 95
The Right Approach to Purchase Orders 96

Pillar #4 Shipping and Logistics 99
Prep Center or Warehouse? Pros and Cons 99
My Experience with Warehouses and Prep Centers 102
How to Choose the Right Warehouse 104
How to Choose the Right Prep Center 106
When to Start Using a Prep Center or Warehouse 108
Shipping Options: SPD Versus LTL/FTL 110
Encouraging Suppliers to Ship Directly to FBA 112
Arranging LTL Shipments 114
Arranging FTL Shipments with Amazon Freight 116
Utilizing 2D Barcodes for Efficient Wholesale Prep 118

Choosing a Credit Card for Shipping Expenses 120
Understanding Shipping Costs to Prevent Leakage 122

Pillar #5 Hiring Virtual Talent 125
Organizational Chart for a Seven-Figure Wholesale Business 125
Hiring Your First Virtual Assistants.. 129
Key VA Performance Indicators to Monitor 131
Where to Find Virtual Assistants 133
Hiring Overseas Versus Domestic 135
Strategies for Disqualifying Candidates 137
Tips for Hiring Outstanding Virtual Assistants 139
Setting Expectations with Virtual Assistants 140
Red Flags to Watch Out for During Hiring 142
Empowering Virtual Assistants to Craft SOPs 144
Lessons Learned from hiring Over 30 Virtual Assistants... 146

Getting Started.. 149
22-Day Action Plan 149
Want More?.. 151
Diving into the Amazon Community on Social Media 152
Thank You 154

From College Grad to Amazon Success: My Journey

Six years ago, I stood in front of my college. I had just graduated and I was ready to take on the world. It felt like only yesterday that I was one of the countless students worried about final exams and dreaming of a big job in a big city. Fast forward to today, and it's astonishing to think that my Amazon wholesale business has generated over $10 million in sales. But how did I get here? This is my story.

In 2017, brimming with enthusiasm, I packed my bags and moved from my home state of North Carolina to the bustling streets of Chicago. An offer from a tech behemoth was too tempting to resist. On the surface, it was a dream job: a role selling data storage for a well-known tech company. The skyscrapers, the high-energy pace, and the rush of being in a metropolitan tech hub—it felt like I was living the dream. Yet, as days turned into months, my excitement began to fade.

Glancing around my workspace, it was awash with stressed faces putting in endless hours. Everyone was striving to ascend the corporate ladder, but they were sacrificing their personal lives in the process. They were putting in 60-hour weeks and missing birthdays, anniversaries, and milestones in their children's lives. I could see their dedication, but there was a budding realization inside me that this life was not sustainable. It definitely didn't look fulfilling. Moreover, the entrepreneurial itch kept rearing its head, and I knew I had to do something about it.

At this point, I had been selling on Amazon for a few months. It was a casual side hustle that I never really took seriously. My initial products? Used books. It was a humble start. I'd scour local thrift stores, hunting for books that cost as little as 50 cents. I'd turn around and resell them on Amazon for $25, $50, sometimes $100 or more. But as I dove deeper into the rabbit hole of selling on Amazon, I stumbled upon the goldmine that was Amazon wholesale.

In 2019, the appeal of wholesale, a business model where I could purchase brand name products directly from manufacturers or authorized distributors for resale, became too strong to resist. The allure of not spending on ads or undergoing the laborious process of product creation appealed to me in a big way. Armed with this newfound knowledge, I took the leap. I left Chicago and my corporate job behind. This was the excuse I needed to finally take a risk and start my own business. I soon found myself back in North Carolina, living with my mother, determined to make Amazon wholesale my full-time gig.

Now, if you're expecting an overnight success story, I'm sorry to burst that bubble. The first few months were grueling. I didn't really make any money. My dwindling savings became a daily stressor. By December 2019, with a mere $1,000 left, desperation took me to Raleigh, NC. There, I found myself working for my uncle's insurance agency, earning $15 an hour. The dream of running a profitable, full-time Amazon business seemed very far away, almost unreachable.

But then, in 2020, as the world grappled with the unforeseen challenges of COVID-19, a silver lining emerged for my Amazon venture. The tides turned. In April 2020, we netted a profit of $5,000, and then the numbers soared: $10,000, $20,000.... It was a roller coaster, and I was holding on for dear life. By August 2020, I found myself at another crossroads, and this time I left the insurance agency, determined to chase the Amazon dream once again.

So, I got to work. And that work started to pay off. During December of that year, in a span of just three weeks, the business profited a whopping $70,000. To put that into perspective, that was more than I had made in a year in my corporate gig. The sense of achievement felt unbelievable.

It's now September 14, 2023. Since I delved into Amazon wholesale, over $10 million worth of brand name products have been sold. What was once a one-man show now employs three incredible people based in the Philippines and Nigeria. They efficiently handle 95% of the day-to-day operations. As of writing this book, I work less than 10 hours a week on my Amazon wholesale business.

The road has been long, filled with trial and error and thousands of cold calls. I've had to analyze tens of thousands of products and invest millions in inventory. But every setback, every hurdle, has shaped this journey. This book is not about boasting, but about illustrating the power of persistence, the magic of the right business model (wholesale), and the vast potential of a platform like Amazon.

In the chapters to follow, I'll be unraveling the secrets and strategies that have brought me Amazon wholesale success. I hope these principles can help light the way for aspiring entrepreneurs like you.

What to Expect in This Book

Welcome to the next step in your Amazon journey. As you delve into the pages of *The 5 Pillars of Amazon Wholesale*, you're not just going to hear about my story. You're going to create your own story. The knowledge you're about to gain has been gleaned from years of experience, some key successes, and many hard-earned lessons. So, without further ado, let's dive into what you can expect from this book.

What You WILL Find in This Book

Stepping into the world of wholesale, especially on a platform as vast as Amazon, can feel daunting. Where do you begin? How do you ensure you're on the right track? This book will be your compass. You'll be provided with a step-by-step blueprint, starting with core concepts you'll need to know and the mindset you'll need to have. It'll lead you through the intricacies of the Amazon wholesale business model and how to set up your very own venture. Every chapter is meticulously designed to guide you through the maze, ensuring you start on a solid foundation. And for those who are entirely new to this realm, rest assured, every concept will be broken down to its simplest form to ensure clarity.

1) **Tested Strategies That Actually Work**

The world of e-commerce is brimming with theories, supposed best practices, and countless how-to guides. The Amazon space is notorious for overpriced courses and mentorships that provide no real value. But here's the difference: the strategies you'll discover in this book aren't mere theories. They are real-world, battle-tested tactics that I have personally used to achieve the results I detailed in my story. From selecting the right products and partnering with reliable brands to scaling past seven figures with Filipino virtual assistants, every strategy is grounded in real experience. This isn't about chasing the next shiny object; it's about proven methods that drive tangible results.

2) Tactical Tips You Can Implement Immediately

While overarching strategies are essential, sometimes what we need are actionable tips that can be put into practice straight away. This book is peppered with tactical nuggets of wisdom that could be your game-changers. Whether it's mastering the art of negotiations with suppliers, optimizing your product listings, or managing your inventory effectively, you'll find specific actions you can take, often in less than 24 hours, that could yield noticeable improvements in your business. These are the little hacks and adjustments that can propel your business from good to outstanding.

3) Principles That Apply Beyond Just Amazon

Yes, this book is about mastering Amazon wholesale, but the principles embedded within its pages transcend this specific model. The core process of building and scaling a business and the universal principles that guide all successful ventures apply to Amazon wholesale the same way they apply to other industries. Thus, while your immediate goal might be to conquer Amazon, the wisdom you'll gain will equip you to succeed in any business landscape. Whether you diversify into other e-commerce platforms in the future, open a brick-and-mortar store, or scale into a global enterprise, the principles you'll learn here will remain your guiding stars.

In essence, *The 5 Pillars of Amazon Wholesale* is more than just a book. It's a mentorship, a roadmap, an education. As you flip through its pages, remember to not just read but to internalize, to not just understand but to implement. Entrepreneurship is more about action than knowledge.

Now that you have clear expectations of what you *will* learn, let me briefly go over what I won't be giving you in this book.

What You WON'T Find in This book

As we journey deeper into the world of Amazon wholesale, it's just as vital to understand the things you will *not* encounter within these pages as it is to know what you will. Clarity is extremely important here, so I want to make sure I'm being as transparent as possible. So, let's dispel some common business book myths and set the record straight about what this isn't designed to do.

1) This Is Not a Get-Rich-Quick Scheme

Let's address the most glaring misconception head-on: this book is not your ticket to instant wealth. It isn't a magical portal where you'll leapfrog over others into overnight success. Yes, the potential in the Amazon wholesale business is vast, and it can be incredibly lucrative. But as with anything worthwhile, it demands dedication, effort, and, most importantly, time. Remember my journey—the trials and tribulations, the setbacks, and the persistence required. Expect to be equipped with the knowledge and tools to succeed, but be ready to put in the hard work.

2) My Personal Rolodex of Suppliers

Building relationships with suppliers is a crucial and personal part of the wholesale business. While I'll provide ample guidance on how to find, approach, and negotiate with suppliers, I won't be handing you a list of my contacts on a silver platter. This isn't out of secrecy, but a belief in the importance of forging your own partnerships and learning through the process. Every entrepreneur's journey is unique, and you'll find suppliers and partners that resonate best with your vision and goals.

3) Untested Theories and Fluff

This book isn't full of hypothetical strategies or unproven theories. Everything in these pages comes from experience. Therefore, if there's a method or tactic that hasn't been put through the wringer, that hasn't been tested in Amazon wholesale, you won't find it here. Every piece of advice, every strategy you see, is grounded in real-world application.

4) A One-Size-Fits-All Approach

Every business, like its owner, is unique. While the strategies and principles in this book have been widely effective, it's crucial to understand that there is no one-size-fits-all approach. You may have more luck working directly with brands while another reader may crush it with distributors. You'll learn to adapt and tweak the strategies here based on your circumstances, your product choices, and your personal business goals.

The Structure of This Book

At the end of each chapter, you'll see a short summary. There are certain elements of what I want to teach you about Amazon wholesale that are not suited to text. For example, several extensive tech tutorials for product sourcing merit different media types. So, for that type of content, we've linked (via QR codes) to private videos created exclusively for the reader. We also outline the steps in the text, but the videos are much easier to follow, and we are able to update them when the format or processes of the tools inevitably change.

There will also be external links throughout the book to resources, recommended tools, and additional materials.

Getting to Grips with Wholesale

What Is Amazon Wholesale?

In the vast ecosystem of e-commerce, there are countless ways to carve out a niche and build a successful business. One of the most lucrative and scalable models within this ecosystem is Amazon wholesale. Whether you're a complete novice dipping your toes in the waters of online selling or an advanced seller seeking to diversify your portfolio, understanding Amazon wholesale can be the key to taking your e-commerce business to the next level. So, let's unravel this model together.

At its core, the Amazon wholesale business model involves purchasing products in bulk from manufacturers or authorized distributors and then selling those products individually on the Amazon marketplace. Unlike private label, where sellers source a product and brand it as their own, or retail arbitrage, where sellers buy retail products at a discount to resell them, the wholesale model centers around creating long-term relationships to access established branded products.

Why Amazon?

Amazon is the 500-pound gorilla in the world of e-commerce, boasting millions of active users and unparalleled logistical capabilities. When you harness the power of Amazon with the wholesale model, you're positioning yourself at the intersection of supply and massive demand. It can be a potential goldmine for entrepreneurs who are able to strategically navigate the platform, and here's why.

Risks vs. Benefits

The Benefits of Amazon

1) Established Brand Recognition

Unlike venturing into private label, you're not starting from scratch. When selling known brands, there's already an established customer base. People recognize the brand, trust it, and are therefore more likely to make a purchase.

2) Economies of Scale

Buying in bulk often results in per-item cost savings. This can lead to improved profit margins, especially when coupled with the massive customer base Amazon provides. These economies of scale apply when buying products in bulk, when shipping products in bulk, when sourcing capital, and in many other parts of the business.

3) Less Marketing Hassle

With established brands, there's less of a need to pour money into advertising and brand-building efforts. Customers are already searching for these products, so you only need to focus on getting them to buy from you.

4) Streamlined Logistics with FBA

By using the Fulfillment by Amazon (FBA) service, sellers can store their products in Amazon's fulfillment centers. Amazon takes care of storage, packaging, and shipping, allowing sellers to scale without getting bogged down in logistics.

The Downsides of Amazon

While the Amazon wholesale model sounds enticing, and has proven lucrative for many, it's not without its challenges. Here are some of the downsides of selling on Amazon.

1) Competition

Given the appeal of selling established brands, many sellers flock to the wholesale model, making some niches fiercely competitive. Establishing genuine relationships with manufacturers and distributors is a way to slant the odds in your favor. These relationships are the protective moat around your business.

2) Price Wars

With multiple sellers offering the same product, there can be a race to the bottom where prices are concerned. This can erode profit margins. Unsophisticated sellers who don't understand their margins may try to undercut you to make a quick sale.

3) Managing Supplier Relationships

Establishing strong relationships with manufacturers and distributors is pivotal. Manufacturers need to trust that you'll represent their brand effectively and maintain its reputation. Distributors need to know you'll be a reliable, consistent customer who adheres to the rules and regulations that their manufacturers set for their brands.

A Glimpse Forward

So, is Amazon wholesale the right model for you? This model, while challenging, offers a clear path to scaling a business on one of the world's largest online marketplaces. It's a model that combines the cachet of established brands with the massive reach of Amazon, a synergy hard to ignore.

For those who can adeptly navigate the challenges, foster strong supplier relationships, and strategically position their listings, the sky is the limit. Over the coming chapters, we'll delve deeper into the nitty-gritty, from sourcing products to mastering the intricacies of the Amazon platform.

But for now, as you ponder over the prospect of starting a business using the Amazon wholesale model, remember that, like all business models, it requires patience, persistence, and a strategic approach. In this vast playground of e-commerce, armed with the right knowledge, you stand poised to make your mark.

The Biggest Sellers in Wholesale

When it comes to Amazon, a marketplace that sees millions of transactions each day, the potential for scaling your business can be astronomical. It's not surprising then that some of the most colossal third-party sellers on Amazon owe their success to the wholesale model. These titans have not only managed to corner vast segments of the market; they have also provided a blueprint for what success can look like when done well.

1) Expertise in Amazon's Ecosystem

These top-tier sellers have mastered the intricacies of Amazon's platform. They understand the algorithm, know how to optimize listings for search visibility, and are proactive in soliciting customer reviews to bolster their seller feedback scores and their product rankings. This expertise allows them to consistently stay ahead of the competition.

2) In-House Branding

While wholesale primarily involves selling established brands, many successful sellers leverage their position to launch in-house brands. For example, 6th Avenue Electronics has successfully introduced its own private label line of products, offering them alongside established brands. This provides them with higher profit margins and greater control over product quality.

3) Robust Logistics and Fulfillment

These sellers don't just rely on FBA. Companies like NetRush have invested in their warehousing and fulfillment infrastructure, ensuring quicker turnaround times and enhanced quality control.

These giants serve as living proof of the potential of the wholesale model on Amazon. They are a testament to the fact that, with the right strategy, it's possible to scale from a modest operation to an e-commerce juggernaut.

However, it's also essential to understand that their success is a result of consistent effort, a willingness to learn and adapt, and an unwavering commitment to delivering value to their customers *and* their suppliers. These companies should serve as inspiration to anyone looking to get involved in the wholesale business. But keep in mind that each person is responsible for charting their own path. The journey to the top is long and requires patience, strategy, and grit.

Approaches to Wholesale

Amazon's vast marketplace offers a plethora of opportunities for sellers. If you're looking to venture into the wholesale domain, it's crucial to understand the various ways in which to approach this business model. Each method comes with its own set of advantages and challenges. Here's a breakdown of the most common approaches to wholesale.

Working with Distributors

Distributors act as intermediaries between manufacturers and retailers. They typically have a broad network of connections and can supply products from various manufacturers. Distributors often purchase products in massive quantities, and this gives them the ability to offer competitive prices.

Here are the benefits of working with distributors.

1) Access to Big Brands

If you're aiming to sell products from household names like Gillette or Nestlé, distributors are your gateway. It's tough to get direct accounts with mega-brands.

2) Scalability

With their vast product range, distributors can quickly help you scale your business.

3) Relationship Benefits

Building a strong relationship with your distributor's sales reps can result in you getting first dibs on new products or exclusive deals.

Here are the drawbacks.

1) Higher Prices (Potentially)

Distributors, being middlemen, can sometimes have higher prices compared to buying directly from brands or certain wholesalers.

2) You're Only as Good as Your Next Order

Distributors only care about one thing: How much money are you going to spend? When working with distributors, you're only as good as your next order.

Working with Wholesalers

Here are the benefits of working with wholesalers.

1) Attractive Prices

Due to the high volumes that wholesalers deal with, they often get products at significantly discounted prices, which they can pass on to you.

2) Profitable Relationships

A trustworthy wholesaler can be a goldmine, offering consistent access to profitable inventory over extended periods.

Here are the drawbacks to working with wholesalers.

1) Risk of IP Complaints

Since many wholesalers aren't authorized sellers of certain brands, you might face IP complaints, even if the products are legitimate.

2) Uncertain Authenticity

There's a higher risk of ending up with counterfeit products when not sourcing directly from a brand or an authorized distributor.

Your choice of suppliers should align with your business goals, risk tolerance, and the level of investment you're willing to make in relationship building. While working directly with brands offers safety and long-term profitability, distributors open doors to mega-brands and quick scaling. On the other hand, wholesalers can offer attractive prices but with higher risks attached.

In the ever-evolving landscape of Amazon wholesale, staying adaptable, conducting thorough due diligence, and focusing on building strong relationships will always remain your top priority, no matter which type of supplier you choose to work with.

Working Directly with the Manufacturer

This approach cuts out the middleman. Here, you're looking to establish a direct relationship with the product maker. This method is most viable when working with small to mid-sized brands. You're unlikely to be able to work directly with a massive manufacturer like Nestlé or Proctor & Gamble, etc.

Here are the benefits of working directly with brands.

1) Safety and Authenticity

There's minimal risk of intellectual property complaints, assuming you're an authorized seller. Your relationship with the brand ensures that you're selling genuine products, so you never have to worry about authenticity claims.

2) Stable Communication

Direct communication with the manufacturer can be invaluable if there are ever any issues with one of their listings or if the brand decides to limit its sellers.

3) Profitability Over Time

Brand-direct accounts can be challenging to secure, but once you're in, they ensure longer-term profits, given the high barriers to entry.

Here are the parts that aren't as appealing.

1) Challenging to Land

It can be time-consuming and challenging to convince brands, especially established ones, to allow you to sell their products.

2) Pricing Variability

While you might expect the best prices from the source, this isn't always the case. Your purchasing volume will dictate the kind of discounts you get.

Creating Branded Bundles

This is a relatively new approach that has gained in popularity in recent years. Branded bundles involve combining multiple products (either similar or complementary) into a single package under your brand name. This approach can differentiate your product offering and add unique value for the customer.

1) **Advantages**

Bundling can set you apart from competitors, potentially leading to higher sales volumes and significantly less competition. This strategy can increase your average order value and help to clear slow-moving stock when paired with popular items.

2) **Challenges**

Bundling requires careful consideration of what products to combine—the combination must make sense to the consumer. Additionally, there's a need for proper branding, packaging, and marketing to ensure the bundle appeals to potential buyers. Logistics and inventory management can also become more complex.

The approach you choose will largely depend on your business goals, available capital, and personal preferences. Whether you opt for working with a distributor, a wholesaler, directly with the manufacturer, or creating branded bundles, each method offers unique opportunities to succeed within the wholesale business model. Do your research. The beauty of Amazon wholesale is that you don't have to be married to one of these approaches. You can start with one, pivot to another, or do them all simultaneously. The choice is yours.

The Importance of Choosing a Niche

In the vast Amazon ecosystem, containing millions of products and millions of brands, the prospect of working out where to start can be daunting. The temptation to dive into multiple categories, hoping to just "sell anything that is profitable," is alluring. However, there's a compelling case for narrowing your focus: choosing a niche. While every category on Amazon has the potential to be profitable, there are several distinct benefits to becoming a specialist in a particular area.

Let's explore the advantages of a niche-centric approach.

1) Fostering Healthy Competition Among Suppliers

When you operate within a niche, you'll quickly discover that many suppliers within the same category are familiar with one another. This familiarity can be leveraged to your advantage. When Supplier A knows you're also getting a quote from Supplier B, it fosters a sense of urgency. They'll recognize the need to offer you the best deals, the most favorable terms, and the most reliable service to secure your business. Remember, you're the buyer. You're the one looking to spend the money. This gives you the upper hand. Use it to secure the best possible deal.

2) Building Trust with Suppliers

Suppliers prefer to deal with people that demonstrate a genuine interest in and understanding of their products. This is especially true when working directly with a manufacturer. When you're niche-focused, it's clear to suppliers that you operate primarily within *their* industry. This specialization is reassuring for them. You aren't just another retailer dabbling in a bunch of different categories without any deep-rooted knowledge. Instead, they'll view you as a dedicated partner, genuinely invested in the industry. This trust can open doors to better deals, early access to new products, and even exclusive partnerships.

Being recognized as an expert can pave the way to landing bigger accounts or securing more exclusive deals. Manufacturers are always on the lookout for partners who can amplify their brand's presence and drive consistent sales. Who is a manufacturer more likely to partner with: an Amazon retailer that sells in many different categories or one that specializes in their product category? Your niche expertise positions you as the ideal candidate for partnerships like these.

3) Establishing Expertise

Perhaps the most important benefit of choosing a niche is the opportunity to become an expert in that category. Over time, as you immerse yourself in the niche, you'll accumulate a wealth of knowledge—about products, industry trends, customer preferences, and more. This expertise gives you a huge competitive advantage.

When you approach new suppliers or manufacturers, this deep understanding of the category speaks volumes. It not only shows your commitment, but it also showcases your potential value as a partner. Suppliers are more inclined to trust a retailer who knows the ins and outs of the industry, as it shows a higher likelihood of sustained sales and growth.

Furthermore, this niche expertise helps you to identify potential gaps in the marketplace. With an intimate understanding of customer needs and preferences on Amazon, you can help educate your suppliers on the types of products you need to source to succeed.

Amazon's marketplace is one of those places where you can sell just about any type of product and make money, but there's undeniable wisdom in choosing a niche. By concentrating your efforts on a specific category, you'll build stronger supplier relationships, get more competitive pricing, and most importantly, establish yourself as an industry expert. This expertise, in turn, becomes your most important asset, facilitating growth, profitability, and long-term success. Remember, in the world of business, depth often trumps breadth. By going deep into a niche, you'll find opportunities that are otherwise hidden to those skimming the surface.

Necessary Tools: A Comprehensive List

The right tools can streamline your Amazon wholesale business, ensuring you're equipped to make informed decisions, optimize your processes, and maximize profits. While some tools are critical, others can be introduced as your business grows. Let's dive deep into some of the top tools every Amazon wholesale seller should consider.

Keepa

Purpose: Keepa is the most important tool in your arsenal. Keepa provides a ton of data about every aspect of a product listing on Amazon. Learning to read a Keepa graph is your top priority as a new seller.

Application: For wholesale sellers, Keepa is indispensable. It provides price history charts for millions of Amazon products. These charts also plot the demand, amount of competition, and fluctuations over time. This data helps you to anticipate demand spikes and understand price trends for products. This can be crucial in determining when to buy and at what price point to sell.

Essentiality: Absolutely essential. Without this insight into historical price points and sales rank, making informed sourcing decisions becomes a game of chance.

SellerAmp

Purpose: SellerAmp helps you analyze products for profitability and easily track thousands of product leads at a time.

Application: At a glance SellerAmp tells you 3 things: *can you sell it? Does it sell? Is it profitable?*

Essentiality: A must-have. You can use Amazon's free FBA fee calculator to analyze products but it takes ten times as long. Trust me, this tool is worth it.

SmartScout

Purpose: This is an advanced product and supplier research tool with a host of benefits for Amazon wholesale sellers.

Application: SmartScout helps you to identify profitable products, discover suppliers, spot new niches, monitor which suppliers are attending trade shows, and so much more. The tool's detailed filter options make it easy to pinpoint items and brands that match your business model.

Essentiality: SmartScout is probably my favorite tool on the market. It's extremely helpful for finding brands to contact, but it is not a necessity on day one.

Seller Snap

Purpose: This is an AI-powered Amazon repricing tool that won't have you racing to the bottom.

Application: Seller Snap analyzes your competition, adjusting your pricing to keep you in the Buy Box as long as possible without drastically undercutting your profits.

Essentiality: As your inventory grows, automated repricing becomes a 100% must. Seller Snap is a premium tool for sellers that are scaling fast.

Seller Investigators

Purpose: Seller Investigators is more of a service than a tool, but one that I believe is essential. Amazon loses or damages your products all the time, and Seller Investigators opens cases with Amazon to get you that money back. They take a small cut of whatever they get for you, so you only pay if they perform.

Application: Seller Investigators keeps an eye on all of your shipments and returns. They proactively ask Amazon for your money back when Amazon makes a mistake. This happens in the background, but sometimes they need paperwork from you (invoices etc.).

Essentiality: This is one of those tools that makes more sense the bigger you get. Seller Investigators has recouped $121,693 for us in the last year. If you're doing a lot of sales, it's a must!

Sellerboard

Purpose: This is an accurate profit analytics service for Amazon sellers.

Application: Sellerboard offers a clear picture of your financials, including profits, losses, and even projections. It accounts for various costs like returns, advertising, and storage to provide genuine profit figures. We use Sellerboard to help us make purchasing decisions.

Essentiality: Your finances can get complex as you scale. Every penny counts. Sellerboard's insights make tracking gross profit a breeze. If you're serious about this business, you'll get Sellerboard sooner rather than later.

Melio

Purpose: This is a tool that allows you to use your credit card to pay suppliers, although they receive cash.

Application: You'll be spending big money in your wholesale business. You want to be doing the bulk of that spend on credit cards for points and cash back. We pay vendors using Melio so we can still get the points.

Essentiality: This isn't essential from the start. Since there's a transaction fee on each payment (2.9%), Melio makes the most sense for higher margin products.

Diving into the world of Amazon wholesale without the right tools is the same as navigating a maze blindfolded. While Keepa and SellerAmp are your compass and map—truly essential from day one—the other tools bring added clarity, efficiency, and more choice on how to approach certain opportunities. Integrate them as your business evolves, ensuring you're always equipped to tackle challenges head on. Your toolkit is an investment; one that pays dividends in the form of insights, time saved, and enhanced profitability. Choose wisely!

Setting Up Your Business Structure

Establishing a successful Amazon wholesale business requires more than just a keen eye for profitable products and strong supplier relationships. You must also create a legitimate business structure. Make sure you commit to establishing a strong foundation from the start. This establishes your credibility with suppliers and customers alike. Here's a detailed breakdown of the structural essentials for launching your Amazon wholesale venture.

Employer Identification Number (EIN)

Description: An EIN is essentially a social security number for your business, assigned by the Internal Revenue Service (IRS). It allows you to file taxes, hire employees, and open business bank accounts. It's also often requested by wholesalers or distributors before they do business with you.

Steps: Getting an EIN is straightforward and free. Simply visit the IRS website and apply online.

Business Entity

Description: Most Amazon sellers lean toward establishing an LLC (limited liability company). It provides a layer of protection between your business and your personal assets. In case of any legal issues or debts, your personal property remains shielded.

Steps: Each state has its process for setting up an LLC. Generally, it involves choosing a unique business name, filing articles of organization, and paying a registration fee.

Business Bank Account

Description: This is a separate account dedicated to your business transactions. It ensures clarity in finances and easier tax filing, and it shows professionalism. Mixing personal and business transactions can lead to auditing nightmares.

Steps: Once you have your EIN and LLC documentation, approach a bank of your choice and open a business bank account.

Professional Email Address

Description: Ditch your generic Gmail or Yahoo address for a domain-specific email. An email from a dedicated domain (e.g., john@yourbusinessname.com) boosts your credibility. Suppliers are more likely to take you seriously, and it underscores your commitment to the business.

Steps: Purchase a domain name and set up an email service through hosting platforms like GoDaddy or Bluehost.

Storefront or Informational Website

Description: While Amazon will be your primary sales channel, having a digital presence outside of it is beneficial. An informational website tells suppliers who you are and what you do. Again, this gives you credibility and instils trust. A storefront website, on the other hand, is an entirely separate sales channel.

Steps: Various platforms like Wix or WordPress work for a basic informational site. Shopify is your best bet for a storefront site.

Customer Relationship Management (CRM)

Description: This is a system to manage your supplier relationships and interactions.

Steps: Please do not overcomplicate this. I want you to track your supplier outreach in a Google sheet. That's it. Add each supplier you contact and note the date you're supposed to follow up with them.

Shipping Address

Description: This is a dedicated address where your inventory is received, prepped, and shipped to Amazon.

Steps: If you're using a prep center (3PL), this becomes your primary shipping address. For those handling inventory themselves, their residential address can serve this purpose initially. If you're receiving inventory at your house, be sure to keep a clear space to work on your business.

Reseller's Permit

Description: Also known as a sales tax permit or certificate, this is obtained from your state's Department of Revenue. It allows you to purchase goods without paying sales tax, given you'll be reselling them. Suppliers often ask for this before establishing a business relationship with you.

Steps: Visit your state's Department of Revenue website and follow their registration process.

Creating a solid structural foundation is essential for any aspiring Amazon wholesale seller. It not only streamlines operations but also positions your business for growth and scalability. While some steps might seem mundane, they collectively contribute to building a reputable, efficient, and profitable wholesale business on Amazon. Start right, and you'll set yourself up for sustainable success.

Core Concepts and Mindset

The Compounding Effect of Wholesale

In the world of business, few things are as exhilarating as witnessing the compounding effects of your efforts. The principle of compounding is typically associated with finance and investment, but in the Amazon wholesale realm, you can experience compounding in multiple areas: capital, relationships, and team growth. Each layer, when nurtured, can lead to exponential returns. Let's delve deeper into its transformative power.

Capital Compounds Quickly

It starts with a simple investment in inventory. Consider this: You've diligently researched the market and have decided to spend $3,000 on a batch of products, confident in the Keepa graph and project profitability. When these items sell, you don't merely recoup your initial investment; you reap profits. Imagine your returns amount to $3,900.

What Now? The Magic Lies in Reinvesting

With that $3,900, you purchase more inventory, perhaps testing out some new products or going deeper with the winners from the first batch. These products then sell for, say, $5,200. This cycle, when repeated, sees your capital not just grow but flourish. With each reinvestment, your purchasing power is amplified, and so is your potential profit.

But remember, the key here is "if you buy right." Market research, understanding the Keepa graph, and sourcing products at the right price are the linchpins of this compounding effect.

Relationships Compound Over Time

As with any business, relationships are pivotal. In the wholesale arena, forming genuine connections with manufacturers and distributors is essential. Initially, your relationships might be transactional, but over time, as trust and reliability are established, the dynamics shift.

A supplier who once offered you a 10% discount might, after a year of consistent business and prompt payments, extend a 20% reduction. Or they might provide you with an exclusive first look at new products, giving you a competitive edge. Deeper relationships often lead to better deals, exclusives, and better credit terms.

Think of it as a mutual growth journey. As your business scales, their sales rise too. It's a symbiotic relationship where success is shared.

Your Team Compounds Over Time

As you expand, so does the need to delegate and hire. As you scale, you might have a handful of employees handling logistics, purchasing, and other operational tasks. As they familiarize themselves with your business processes, their efficiency improves.

The first year might see them grappling with the nuances of the Amazon platform, supplier interactions, or inventory management. But by the third year? They're likely managing these tasks with ease, foreseeing challenges, and implementing solutions without needing your intervention.

Moreover, as they grow within the company, they can mentor newer hires, passing on their expertise. This cascading effect ensures that your business runs smoother, faster, and more efficiently. The best employees not only save you time but also become invaluable assets, driving growth and innovation.

The beauty of the Amazon wholesale model is its potential for rapid scaling. And this is about exponential and not just linear growth. Your initial capital, when invested correctly, will multiply. The relationships you nurture today can lead to more profitable deals tomorrow. And the team you build will become the backbone, supporting and propelling your business vision.

In essence, the compounding effect in Amazon wholesale isn't just about numbers; it's self-propelling growth where every element—be it capital, relationships, or team—feeds into and amplifies the other. As with all compound effects, the key is patience and consistent effort. The rewards, as many successful sellers will tell you, are well worth the journey.

Setting Expectations: The Mindset for Success in Amazon Wholesale

The world of Amazon wholesale is vast and full of potential. It's a platform where dreams of financial independence and entrepreneurship come to fruition. However, like any business that promises great rewards, it demands its due in dedication, patience, and strategic thinking. Let's break down the mindset and expectations you need to cultivate to not only survive but thrive in this competitive arena.

It's a Marathon, Not a Sprint

While success stories about Amazon sellers might paint a picture of overnight riches, the reality is often far from this. Every single triumph you've seen in the Amazon wholesale world is built on years of perseverance. Many seasoned sellers agree that it's the persistent grind between the second and the fifth year that cements a business's foundation and often proves to be the turning point. The initial years are about understanding the landscape, making mistakes, learning, and iterating.

If you step into this world expecting instant results, prepare for failure. But if you're ready to see this as a marathon, pacing yourself and learning with each lap, there might just be a trophy waiting for you at the finish line.

Consistency Over Intensity

Diving headfirst into your venture and working 12-hour days might seem like the quickest path to success. But while short bursts of intense work are valuable, they aren't sustainable. Rather, envision your journey like dripping water eroding a path through rock. It's not the force but the consistent dripping that, over time, makes an impact.

Committing two hours daily to your business can lead to more systematic growth. It helps you to embed a daily sourcing practice and regular check-ins on inventory and sales metrics, as well as maintain consistent communication with suppliers. This consistency means you're in tune with the pulse of your business, making timely decisions and growing steadily.

Human Connection: Your Underrated Asset

The digital age, with all its convenience, often makes us forget the power of human connection. In Amazon wholesale, emails and digital communication tools are essential, but they're just the tip of the iceberg. True growth comes when you dive deeper, establishing and nurturing relationships with key suppliers, service providers, and even other sellers.

Picking up the phone and calling a supplier, attending trade shows, or even visiting manufacturers can give you an edge in this business. Personal interactions foster trust and mutual understanding, and they often lead to better deals and insider insights. Remember, behind every email address and screen is a person. Recognizing and valuing that person can be your secret weapon in this business.

Reinvest to Rise

One of the most common missteps new Amazon sellers make is cashing in too soon. While seeing profits is exciting and often validates your hard work, the growth trajectory in Amazon wholesale is significantly amplified when you reinvest these profits.

Think of your earnings as seeds. Instead of consuming them, plant them. You can take a little bit off the top for yourself, but keep most of your profits in the business. This means buying more inventory, exploring new niches, investing in tools and resources, and perhaps even expanding your team. The more you reinvest, especially in the early years, the quicker and sturdier your business tree grows.

Success in Amazon wholesale is about much more than understanding the platform and having capital. It's about cultivating a mindset—one of patience, consistency, human connection, and strategic reinvestment. It's about understanding that while the journey might be long and demanding, the destination promises rewards that are not just financial but that also offer personal growth and satisfaction. If you set your expectations correctly and commit to the journey, the world of Amazon wholesale might just be the adventure of a lifetime.

Capital Requirements

The golden question on many potential sellers' minds is: How much do I need to start? In other words, what should your initial capital be? While this may differ based on a number of factors, most sellers would agree that $5,000 is a solid starting point. This might sound like a hefty sum for some, but here's the rationale.

Security and Diversification

With $5,000, you have the flexibility to invest in a range of products. This diversification can be a precaution against risks associated with relying heavily on a single product or two. Having a substantial amount in the bank also provides a cushion against potential unforeseen challenges.

Scaling

If your initial buys perform well, having capital at hand allows you to quickly restock or explore new profitable brands, leading to quicker scaling.

While stories float around of sellers who began with less and still found success, it's essential to understand that such cases are usually exceptions rather than the rule. Starting with at least $5,000 provides a foundation strong enough to withstand the initial hiccups and uncertainties of the Amazon wholesale world.

Budgeting for Education

Knowledge is power, especially in a domain with as much nuance as Amazon wholesale. But acquiring this knowledge often comes at a price. This might be in the form of courses, training programs, seminars, books, or other educational resources. It's tempting to dip into your initial capital for these, but here's a word of caution: don't!

Your $5,000 starting capital is your inventory war chest. Every dollar from this should be dedicated to products, ensuring you maximize the potential returns. Instead, consider educational expenses as separate investments in your business education. This distinction ensures you're financially prepared to both learn and operate.

Capital Versus Time

Money has a unique relationship with time in business, particularly in the initial stages. If you're starting on the lower end of the capital spectrum, expect to invest more time. This is because certain conveniences and efficiencies come at a cost.

For instance, various software tools can automate and streamline operations. However, with limited capital, it might be more economical to manually handle certain tasks initially. As profits roll in and your capital increases, you can then invest in these tools, buying back your time and focusing on strategic expansion.

The less capital you begin with, the more hands-on and time-intensive your operations will be. It's a balance every entrepreneur must strike based on their unique circumstances. As your business grows and becomes more profitable, you can gradually reinvest to enhance operational efficiencies.

Capital is the lifeblood of your Amazon wholesale venture. It's not just about having money; it's about managing and allocating it wisely. Starting with a strong financial footing, like the recommended $5,000, can be a game-changer, providing you with the flexibility, security, and potential for swift scaling. Coupled with a clear division of capital for educational expenses and an understanding of the capital-time relationship, you're setting yourself up for a structured and strategic journey in the Amazon wholesale universe.

Expected Margins

Profitability is the barometer of success in any business, and Amazon wholesale is no exception. However, understanding what margins you can expect in this business is crucial for setting realistic financial goals and ensuring your business can be sustainable over time. Here's a comprehensive look at typical margin levels and the factors that influence them.

Gross Margins

In an Amazon wholesale business, gross margins typically range between 10-20%. This means that after deducting the cost of goods sold (COGS) from your revenue, you're left with 10-20% of the sales amount. It might not sound like a large number, but in the world of wholesale, where volume often compensates for thin margins, it can translate to a large gross profit figure.

Direct from Manufacturer vs. Distributors vs. Wholesalers

While it's commonly believed that buying directly from the manufacturer can yield higher margins, this is not set in stone. Some manufacturers can provide a consistent pricing structure, making margins predictable. However, distributors sometimes offer better deals, especially if they are looking to offload inventory quickly. Additionally, wholesalers can also provide excellent pricing, especially for huge bulk buys. The key takeaway? Always explore multiple sourcing avenues to maximize your margins.

Including the Cost of Capital

If you've borrowed money to fund your inventory, this needs to be accounted for in your margins. Loans or credit lines come with interest rates, and this becomes an additional cost for your business operation. Not factoring in the cost of capital when calculating your margins can give you a skewed perception of your profitability.

Net Margins

After accounting for all business expenses (like operating costs, salaries, marketing, storage, and interest on borrowed capital), if you're left with a net margin of around 10%, consider that a success. Most Amazon wholesale sellers operate within the 5-8% net margin range. These figures might look modest but remember, in a high-volume business such as Amazon wholesale, even single-digit net margins can lead to sizable profits.

Salary Considerations

A common mistake in many new businesses is not accounting for the owner's salary. Many business owners operate under the notion that a $100,000 annual profit implies success. But what if those same business owners didn't take a single dime in salary over the whole year. Make sure that you're not working for free. As soon as it's financially viable, start paying yourself an appropriate salary and account for it when calculating your net margins.

Understanding the margins that you can expect in Amazon wholesale is critical for long-term success. It's not just about calculating the difference between your buying and selling prices but comprehending the various factors that influence these figures. From sourcing options to the cost of capital and operating expenses, numerous variables come into play. Being informed about these not only helps you to set achievable financial goals but also provides you with a clearer picture of your business's health. With the right approach and diligence, you can navigate the financial landscape of Amazon wholesale effectively, ensuring your venture isn't just profitable but also sustainable and scalable.

Building Relationships in the Business

In any business venture, relationships are often the backbone holding every piece of the business in place. This holds especially true in the world of Amazon wholesale, a business model inherently built on partnerships, trust, and mutual growth. Here, relationships are not just a byproduct of doing good business; they are the very foundation on which successful wholesale businesses are built.

Supplier Relationships

Consider your suppliers as your business allies. They are the gatekeepers to the products you need. Maintaining a good relationship with them can be the difference between getting the best deals or being left out in the cold. More than just timely payments and keeping your promises, building a relationship with suppliers often involves open communication, mutual respect, and an understanding of each other's goals.

In my experience, a few solid relationships can make all the difference. We've been able to scale to multiple millions in annual revenue with just six key suppliers—all of whom we've had relationships with for at least two years. These suppliers offer us special pricing, keep us in the loop about new products, and often go above and beyond to meet our needs. This didn't happen overnight; it was cultivated.

Relationships with Other Sellers

One of the biggest mistakes new sellers make is to assume that other Amazon sellers are only competitors. While this is true in many cases, they can also be invaluable allies. Sharing experiences and insights about the Amazon marketplace can help you avoid costly mistakes and even point you toward profitable opportunities. More seasoned sellers can offer advice and strategies that you might not have considered. Some sellers even go into collaborative ventures, pooling their money to get better pricing or sharing warehouse space to lower costs.

Service Provider Partnerships

As you scale, you'll likely start to work with various service providers, be it freight and logistics companies, software providers, or bankers/financial advisors. These relationships are also crucial. Quality service providers not only help your business operate smoothly but can become sources of invaluable industry knowledge and connections.

The Dividends of Good Relationships

The benefits of nurturing these relationships can't be understated. The right supplier can give you an edge in pricing and product availability, allowing you to beat your competitors on Amazon. Long-term relationships might lead to exclusive deals with manufacturers or first dibs on new inventory. With other sellers, you might get tips on high-performing niches, pricing strategies, or even recommendations for trustworthy service providers. Strong relationships with service providers can mean better deals, faster service, and occasionally, useful business referrals.

The Long-Term Perspective

Relationships are not built overnight, and they aren't a one-way street. What you bring to the table matters as much as what you gain. Being reliable, professional, and genuine in your interactions not only secures your place as a preferred buyer or partner; it also uplifts your reputation in the market. And keep in mind that Amazon wholesale is a relatively small niche in the greater e-commerce landscape. Your reputation means everything, and it'll follow you around. Don't burn bridges, and build for the long-term.

In an Amazon wholesale business, the products you sell are important, but the relationships you build are pivotal. They are your support system, your knowledge base, and often, your competitive advantage. Each relationship you cultivate should be viewed as a long-term investment that can pay huge dividends. And remember, in business and in life, people don't just invest in products or services; they invest in people. Make sure you're someone worth investing in.

Pillar #1 Finding Suppliers

Comparing Brands, Distributors and Wholesalers

Choosing Brands to Sell: A Checklist

In the world of Amazon wholesale, making the right choice when it comes to the brands you sell can be the difference between thriving and merely surviving. Many sellers think that targeting popular, well-known brands is the secret to success. In reality, the key lies in identifying smaller to mid-sized niche brands that have less competition, and therefore more potential. Let's delve into our unique "brand checklist," the set of criteria we use to evaluate potential brands to partner with.

#1 There's Existing FBA Competition on Listings

At a glance, this might seem counterintuitive. Why would we actively seek out competition? The logic is simple.

If there are existing third-party sellers selling these brands via FBA, it signals that the brand is open to third-party collaboration. This is a good starting point, since so many brands are selective or even restrictive about who sells their products on Amazon.

Competition is not just a sign that the brand is open to offers—it also implies profitability. If there's existing competition, then those sellers are buying that brand profitably from *somewhere*.

A good rule of thumb is at least *two to three FBA sellers per listing.*

#2 You're Not Competing with Amazon

Amazon, besides being a platform, is also a giant seller. And competing directly with Amazon can be daunting.

When Amazon sells a product, they often dominate the Buy Box—the primary "Add to Cart" option that appears on an Amazon product page—making it challenging for third-party sellers to get visibility.

While we generally avoid brands where Amazon is a dominant seller, there are exceptions. If Amazon shares the Buy Box with third-party sellers, then there's potential to make money on that listing.

Ideally, we want to see Amazon on a listing for *less than 50% of the previous year*. Again, this is a general rule of thumb and there are always exceptions.

#3 The Products Have Existing Demand on Amazon

Brand recognition outside of Amazon doesn't always translate to sales on the platform. Because of this, we focus on brands that already have a built-in demand on Amazon.

I always tell folks to look for products that are "selling well." However, "selling well" is subjective and will depend on your experience in the business. A new seller may jump at the chance to sell a brand that moves 100 units a month, while a seasoned seller may not look at any brands selling less than 1,000 units a month.

Decide where your comfort level lies and go for brands that will move the needle in your business. A good rule of thumb is to target products selling *at least 100 units per month*. As always, there are plenty of exceptions to the rule.

You can spin your wheels for months contacting brands that aren't a good fit. If you want to set yourself up for maximum success and have the highest possible conversion rate, keep this checklist in mind. Remember, it's not about chasing every opportunity; it's about chasing the right ones.

Choosing Distributors to Work With: A Checklist

In the wild world of Amazon wholesale, working with authorized distributors is a fantastic way to access many different brands from the same supplier. Distributors can continue feeding your business over time, ensuring a consistent supply of products and contributing to the growth of your business. It's important to know which distributors align with your business as an Amazon wholesale seller and which don't. To streamline this process, let's dive into this essential checklist for choosing a distributor. Make sure that any distributors you're considering working with meet not just one or two but all the following criteria.

#1 They're 100% B2B (Business-To-Business)

When evaluating distributors, make sure your sights are set on companies that are strictly B2B (business-to-business). This is an important point because many companies call themselves "distributors" yet will sell to anyone. B2B-focused distributors deal exclusively in bulk, offering competitive pricing for large wholesale purchases. Your business model will thrive on obtaining products at the lowest prices, and aligning with B2B distributors helps you meet this goal.

#2 They Carry Brand-Name Products That Already Sell Well on Amazon

Target distributors who sell established brand-name products with built-in demand on Amazon. This approach allows you to leverage existing demand, eliminating the need to launch new products from scratch. If a distributor's inventory is filled with private label products or generic items, the chances of them meeting the criteria are slim.

#3 They Cater to Retailers

A distributor's client base is another pivotal factor. Prioritize those that mainly sell to retailers. Many distributors meet the first two criteria, but they may focus on serving non-retail companies like schools or hospitals. Distributors like these won't be a great fit since you don't fit the "mold" of their typical customer.

For instance, we reached out to a distributor a couple of years ago and ran into this exact issue. Despite being B2B and carrying brand-name products (meeting our first two criteria), their primary customers were schools, hospitals, and government entities. Because we didn't look like one of their typical customers, they denied our account. This highlights the importance of working with distributors where your business mirrors their typical customer profile.

Verify every supplier lead against these criteria. Doing so will drastically increase the chances of it being a profitable relationship.

Finding Brand-Direct Leads with SmartScout

It's all well and good having a checklist to assess the suitability of brands, but you need to go about finding those leads in the first place. In the next few chapters, I've outlined some of the key methods of attack we use to find the best leads in the shortest time possible.

Finding solid brands to sell in your Amazon business can seem daunting, but with tools like SmartScout, you can make the process ten times easier. When looking for brand-direct leads, the ability to efficiently analyze and sort through data is crucial. SmartScout has multiple features tailored for this, providing detailed insights that simplify the path to finding viable opportunities.

SmartScout is a comprehensive tool for Amazon sellers, offering a wide range of features for scouting brands, analyzing competition, and assessing product categories. The tool's robust filtering options allow sellers to hone in on brands that align with their specific criteria, saving them time and ensuring a more targeted approach.

Step #1 Navigate to Brands

Start by accessing the "Brands" function within SmartScout. This feature is designed to help you explore and identify potential brands to work with, offering an extensive database and numerous filtering options.

Step #2 Use Smart Filters

To narrow down the brand options, you'll utilize the "Smart Filters." Select the "Category" filter and choose the desired product category. Clicking "Search" will yield tens of thousands of brand results, but to refine this further, you'll want to set additional filters for certain columns.

The Smart Filters will return tens of thousands of brands in a given category. We'll need to further refine our results so as to increase our chances of success.

Step #3 Adjust the Amazon In Stock Rate

Adjust the "Amazon in stock rate" to a maximum of 60%. This metric is based on the last 90 days and averaged across all the product listings for a given brand. By setting a 60% cap we eliminate most brands that are dominated by Amazon.

Step #4 Adjust Average Number of Sellers

Set the average number of sellers to a minimum of three. This step helps filter out private label brands, which typically have one or two sellers per listing, and ensures you are focusing on brands that allow third-party resellers.

Step #5 Adjust Monthly Revenue Estimate

Set the monthly revenue estimate to a range of a minimum of $30,000 and a maximum of $300,000. Tailor these numbers based on your experience and capacity. Newer sellers might find more opportunities with smaller brands, while seasoned sellers might prefer targeting brands with higher revenue.

Verifying Brand Criteria

After setting these filters, you'll find that the number of results is cut from tens of thousands down to a couple of thousand or maybe even a few hundred, depending on the size of the category. At this point, you'll need to verify each brand further. Open each brand in a new tab to ensure they align with the brand checklist outlined earlier. Despite SmartScout's sophisticated filtering, manual verification ensures that the selected brands indeed meet your specific criteria, enhancing the accuracy of your search.

This detailed process may seem extensive, but see it as a shrewd investment of time and effort, laying the groundwork for the sustainable growth and success of your Amazon wholesale business. We emphasize proper verification on the front end to make sure you don't waste time spinning your wheels—like I did for years—contacting brands that you have no chance of working with.

Finding Brand-Direct Leads Using Amazon's Website

While using tools like SmartScout can drastically cut down the time you spend finding brand-direct leads, it's entirely possible, and free, to use Amazon's website for the same purpose. Though this method will take considerably longer, it's an approach that is just as effective, especially for those starting with a limited budget.

Here's what the process looks like.

Step #1 Choose a Product Category

Begin by navigating to Amazon.com. Choose a product category that you'd like to source. For instance, select "Garden & Outdoors" if you wish to explore brands in this category.

Step #2 Select a Subcategory

Dive in further by choosing a subcategory. Continuing the example above, choose "Gardening Tools." Since we don't have access to advanced filters like we do with SmartScout, this prevents us from digging through millions of different products to find the ones that meet our criteria.

Step #3 Set Filters

You'll now be on the product results page. Though it's optional, setting filters can streamline your search. Opt for a minimum of four stars in customer reviews to ensure you're looking at quality products. Set a minimum price of $20 to filter out low-cost items. This focuses your search on products with potentially higher margins.

Step #4 Utilize DS Amazon Quick View

Download the free Chrome extension, DS Amazon Quick View. This extension shows you, at a quick glance, the sales rank and the number of FBA sellers on each listing, as well as whether or not Amazon is on the listing. This provides a snapshot of the competition and demand for each product.

Step #5 Scan the Listings

Scroll through the search results, keeping an eye out for listings that seem to align with the brand checklist outlined earlier. This step involves attention to detail, ensuring that you only shortlist the most promising leads.

Step #6 Set Aside Potential Leads

Open listings that appear to meet the brand checklist in a new tab for a more in-depth examination.

Step #7 Verify Against the Brand Checklist

Thoroughly analyze each listing to confirm that it meets our brand checklist. Check the number of sellers, the listing history via Keepa, and other pertinent details to make an informed decision. Don't skip this step as it will save you time by avoiding brands that won't be a good fit for your business.

Step #8 Rinse and Repeat

Apply this strategy across any category and subcategory you're interested in selling. Though time-consuming, this approach maximizes your chances of finding suitable brands to work with.

Finding brand-direct leads on Amazon's website is a painstaking yet cost-effective strategy for those with a small amount of starting capital. This hands-on approach also grows your understanding of the Amazon marketplace, equipping you with insights and experience that will come in handy in your Amazon wholesale journey.

Approach this method with patience and persistence. It's not uncommon to go a while without finding leads and then find multiple solid leads on one page. This is the trench work required to grow a profitable and sustainable business.

Finding Brand-Direct Leads by Spying on Other Sellers

One of the most effective strategies for finding promising brand leads is to target your competition, a technique termed "storefront stalking." This method enables you to find products that other sellers have already sourced to identify additional products that meet the brand checklist. Below is a step-by-step guide to this approach.

Step #1 Start with Any Product

Start this process by finding any potential product that meets the brand checklist.

Step #2 Navigate to the Seller's Storefront

Click to view all the offers on a particular product listing. We want to see every seller that is on the listing to find the ones that we want to drill into. Click on their seller name and that will bring up their storefront where you'll see their company information and feedback score.

Step #3 Focus on Specific Sellers

Target sellers with a 30-day feedback score ranging from 100 to 700. This range typically includes sellers following the wholesale business model as they're not mega-sellers operating on thin margins nor are they newer sellers with minimal inventory.

Step #4 Browse Their Inventory

Click through to their storefront to explore the products they carry. Here you'll see every active listing in their storefront. Begin by working down the list.

Step #5 Open Potential Products

Open products in new tabs that seem to align with the brand checklist. Don't analyze products one by one; instead, wait until you have five or more tabs open to batch your analysis.

Step #6 Reconfirm Against the Brand Checklist

For each product opened in a new tab, reconfirm that it aligns with the brand checklist. This step is crucial because if they do, you can storefront stalk the sellers on that listing too.

Step #7 Repeat the Process

You can repeat this process for every new listing you find that meets the brand checklist.

"Storefront stalking" is a savvy approach to finding brand leads by leveraging the existing research of other successful sellers. And keeping a close eye on the competition can open up opportunities that you may have missed.

Approach this technique with a commitment to adhering to the brand checklist. This will make sure you only target brands that are likely to work with you. This is my personal favorite sourcing method as it can provide virtually limitless leads for you or your team to pursue.

Finding Brand-Direct Leads Using Google

In the realm of Amazon wholesale, working with distributors that meet the distributor checklist is incredibly important. A well-crafted Google search can result in finding many potential partners. Here's a guide to harnessing the power of Google to pinpoint distributors that align with your criteria.

Step #1 Initiate Your Google Search

Begin by navigating to Google. Use a broad search format, entering the category name, followed by "distributor," and your city or town. For example, type "kitchenware distributor New York." This specific approach will keep the search results narrow.

Step #2 Experiment with Search Terms

Creativity is important here. Alternate your search terms, experimenting with combinations like "category name wholesale supplier your state." This diversifies your search results, making it more likely you'll find overlooked distributors that align with your criteria.

Step #3 Bypass Sponsored Results

Steer clear of the sponsored results. These companies often target newer retailers and usually don't meet the distributor checklist.

Step #4 Thoroughly Explore Search Results

Don't just stop at the end of page one. Many times, the best suppliers are buried on page two, five, or 10 of Google results. Open potential distributor websites in new tabs for further analysis.

Step #5 Utilize Directories

During your search, keep an eye out for directories that list multiple distributors in a specific category. While some directories are a complete waste of time, others are goldmines that contain multiple legitimate distributors that meet our checklist. In this way, you'll be able to identify many leads at once.

Step #6 Leverage Google Maps

Pay attention to the Google Maps results. Local companies, displayed based on your location and search terms, may be hidden gems.

Now that you have multiple potential supplier websites open in new tabs, it's time to verify them against our distributor checklist. This analysis is critical. It weeds out the bad leads and highlights the great ones.

I want you to prioritize local suppliers. Suppliers that are close by allow for in-person meetings, laying the foundation for a strong partnership from the get-go. Personal interactions like these, sometimes with sales representatives and sometimes with company owners, solidify the relationship much more quickly than digital communication. This can lead to better deals and bigger opportunities down the road.

Searching for qualified distributors may seem daunting. A structured approach leveraging Google can dramatically simplify this process. Remember to use different search terms, avoid sponsored results, verify each potential website against our distributor checklist, and prioritize local suppliers for that personal touch.

Finding Brand-Direct Leads Using SpyFu

Let's talk about another easy way to find suppliers. The tool we're using is called SpyFu. It's an SEO tool and it's completely free. The funny part is we're not using it for SEO. We use it to plug in our existing suppliers and SpyFu gives us website names of similar companies. SpyFu is basically giving us more leads for free. Here's how it works:

Step #1 Go to SpyFu.com

First, we need to go to the website www.spyfu.com.

Step #2 Search for the Distributor

Next, think about a qualified distributor lead that you've already found. Type the website of that distributor in the big search bar on SpyFu, and then click on the search button.

Step #3 Look for Organic Competitors

Now, we scroll down on the page until we find a section called "Organic Competitors." This section shows us other websites that are similar to the one we searched for.

Step #4 Check Each Website

We're going to click on all of these websites. Each one will open in a new tab on our computer. Now, we need to look at each distributor and run it against our distributor checklist. Remember the rules we talked about before? It's the same process.

Step #5 Repeat the Process

If we find a new distributor that meets our criteria, we can follow the same steps again for their website. We go back to SpyFu, type in the new website, and look at the organic competitors. This means we can keep finding more and more distributors!

Finding Distributors by Spotting Local Opportunities

Sometimes, the best ways are the old ways. There's a super helpful method for finding distributors that many people forget about. Your local area will have distributors that might be a perfect fit for you. You just need to find them, analyze their suitability, and knock on their door.

Noticing Opportunities and Knocking on Doors

Guess what? Every day, you'll see trucks on the roads and you'll walk by buildings. Some of these belong to distributors. You might be passing by potential distributors every single day without even noticing! Whether you're driving to work, going to the store, or just taking a walk, keep your eyes peeled for signs or trucks that say "distributor" or "wholesaler" on them.

Every time you see one, write down the name. It's as easy as that. You don't have to go anywhere special. Just keep your eyes open during your regular day.

I tried this myself, and you won't believe it. In just one day, I found five potential local suppliers! I was just driving down the highway, minding my own business. Then I noticed a distributor truck driving by. I wrote down the name, and then I noticed another, and another! By the time I got home, I had five names written down. All from just paying attention while I was driving!

After you write down the name, use Google to look them up. You can usually find their contact information easily. And guess what? Since their trucks are driving around your area, they're probably local. That means you can likely meet them face-to-face. As I've said before, meeting your suppliers face-to-face is the best way to build a strong relationship quickly.

Also, every town or city in America usually has a warehouse district. It's the area filled with big buildings where things are made or stored. And guess what? A lot of those buildings are distributors!

Some of these local distributors might not have a website. They might not even be on social media. So, the only way we can find them is by walking right up to their warehouse. It might seem a bit scary, but it's actually pretty simple and can work really well.

What you do is just walk up to the warehouse and knock on the door. Just like that! Ask to talk to a sales rep. This is a quick way to get in front of the right people at the company. It's much faster than calling or emailing them and waiting for a reply.

A Success Story

Let me tell you a story about a friend of mine. This friend was looking for his first distributor. As I suggested above, he walked up to a big distributor's warehouse in his town and knocked on the door. Simple, right? Well, guess what? It worked!

He got to sit down and talk with a sales rep right then and there. They talked about what he needed and what they could do for him. And you know what happened next? He got the account! He was able to place his first order with the supplier within a week.

Now he orders from them all the time. And because he met his sales rep face-to-face, they have a solid relationship. One that would've taken weeks to build over the phone or email. All of this happened because he decided to just walk up and knock on the door.

Sometimes Simple Is Best

This method is a hidden gem. It's so simple, but it works so well. When you start to look for distributors in your home town, you'll begin to see them everywhere. And in meeting them face-to-face, we build rapport that much faster. They can see who we are, and we can see who they are. It's a quick way to build trust and start a good working relationship.

So, what's the lesson here? Sometimes, we just need to get out there and do the work. It's called pounding the pavement. It might take time, and it will take effort, but it's worth it. However, 99.9% of people aren't willing to put in this kind of work. Are you?

If you're trying to find distributors, don't forget about your local area. Keep an eye out in your daily routine. It'll soon become second nature. Take a walk, knock on some doors, and meet some people. You never know, your next big distributor could be just a short walk away!

And remember the story of my friend. He took a chance, and now he has a great partnership for his business. Someone that he works with all the time. So, why not give it a try? It just might work for you too!

Finding Leads Through Trade Show Exhibitor Lists

This is an excellent and undervalued method of finding lots of potential brand and distributor leads quickly. You can do this by looking through trade show exhibitor lists. The best part about this method is that you don't even need to attend the trade show to make it work, yet you can still gather lots of information. Let's talk about how this works.

Step #1 Choose a Trade Show

First, choose a trade show. You can choose a niche trade show (for example, one catering to fly fishing) or you can choose a broad trade show that is likely to have many different niches represented (ASD, for example, which is a biannual trade show in Las Vegas for all types of suppliers, from fragrances and beauty to tools and kitchenware). You can find trade shows by searching online. Just type the niche you're looking for and "trade show" into a search engine. You can also use AI tools like ChatGPT to brainstorm trade shows in a certain niche or part of the country.

Step #2 Find the Exhibitor List

Next, go to the trade show's website. Look for the exhibitor list. This list has the names of companies that will have booths at the show. The great thing about talking to exhibitors is the reason they attend the show is to sell products. So, if you reach out, express an interest in their products, and mention that you saw them on a trade show's exhibitor list, they'll likely be receptive.

Some trade show websites might make you register to see the exhibitor list. This is usually free, and it's worth it to get access to the list.

Step #3 Go Through the List

Now, go through the list. Write down the names of companies that look like they might be a good fit for you. You can often find their contact information and website on the exhibitor list. If their contact information isn't listed, simply Google their name. You can also do a LinkedIn search for salespeople at the company and reach out to them there. This has been a very effective strategy in our business.

Step #4 Check the Websites

Visit the websites of the companies you wrote down. If it's a brand, check if they fulfil the brand checklist. If it's a distributor, check the distributor checklist. This step ensures you won't waste your time contacting suppliers of generic products or brands that don't have existing demand on Amazon. Take your time going through the list and checking websites. This method is an easy one, but being careful and thorough is important.

Step #5 Repeat as Needed

You can do this as many times as you want. Every trade show has an exhibitor list, and there are lots of trade shows happening all the time. You can go as deep into a niche as you want or as broad into a main category as feels comfortable.

Trade shows are where companies go to find people to sell their products to. They're already looking for customers, which makes your job easier. Even if you can't go to the trade show, the exhibitor list is a treasure chest of leads. Some trade shows have hundreds (some of them thousands) of exhibitors. It's not unheard of to find 20, 30, even 50 or more qualified supplier leads from a single trade show exhibitor list.

Using trade show exhibitor lists is a clever way to find lots of leads without traveling or spending money. Just find a trade show, look at the exhibitor list, and start searching. Remember to check each company against the criteria to make sure they're a good fit. Happy hunting!

Finding Leads by Attending Trade Shows

If you want to take the strategy from the last chapter to the next level, try attending a trade show in person. It's basically one huge sourcing opportunity where you can network with other sellers as well as many qualified vendors, all in one place. Trade shows have a massive ROI when you approach them the right way. Let's explore how you can best navigate a trade show and benefit from your time there.

Trade shows offer so many benefits that you simply can't get anywhere else:

1) Meet People Face-to-Face

It gives you the opportunity to get in front of different vendors in a face-to-face setting which you can't get anywhere else. This gives each of you a better feel for the needs of the other business.

2) Make Quick Deals

If you see a good deal, you can pull the trigger on the spot. This shows vendors that you're serious and immediately enhances your credibility.

3) Get Special Deals

Some companies offer discounts that you can only get at the trade show.

4) Compare Prices

It allows you to see what different companies are charging for similar things, so you can choose the best deal. We've had luck getting concessions from vendors when another vendor is offering the same product at a cheaper price a few booths down.

5) Make New Friends

You can meet other sellers that you can collaborate with and share strategies.

6) Spend Time with Companies

The rapport building benefits of trade shows are unmatched. Apart from meeting suppliers at the show, you get the opportunity to spend time with them socially,

It's important to be strategic in your preparation and approach to trade shows to make the most out of them. The following tips will help you get ready for the show and take advantage of opportunities while you're there.

#1 Do Your Homework

Do some research beforehand and decide which companies you absolutely must talk to. Make a shortlist of these in advance so you can be strategic about your efforts.

Better yet, have some brands and products in mind that you're looking to source while you're there.

#2 Have a Plan, but Be Flexible

Some of our best relationships came about as chance encounters at trade shows. You want to stick to your plan but be open to the opportunities all around you and talk to as many people as possible while you're there.

#3 Know What You Want

Have a clear idea of the brands you're interested in. Ideally, you'd know, down to product level, what you're looking for. This shows vendors you're serious and will help guide your efforts at the show, which can be overwhelming if you walk in without a plan.

#4 Be Ready to Make Decisions

Be ready to pull the trigger if you stumble upon a great deal. This shows vendors you mean business. Disqualify vendors quickly. If a vendor doesn't seem like a good fit for your business, disengage and move onto the next supplier.

#5 Take Good Notes

Taking detailed notes at the show is something most people don't do, but I think it's a vital part of the process. Each time you leave a conversation, make a note of who you talked to, their company, what you spoke about, the types of products they carry, and any other relevant information. I use either the Notes app on my phone or the Voice Memo app. I'll then transcribe these notes into our CRM when I get home from the show.

#6 Don't Forget to Follow Up

This is arguably the most important step in the entire process. Vendors at trade shows have hundreds of conversations per day. I guarantee they will not remember you unless you placed a big order. The key is staying in front of them after the show. Follow up with an email, a phone call, or a text, and let them know you're still interested in any deals they have that meet your criteria. Follow up early and often for the best chance of doing long-term business with them.

#7 Plan Your Dinners

Book a table at a nice restaurant before you go to the show. You can cancel the reservation at any time, but by having one in advance, you give yourself the opportunity to get in front of a vendor outside of the trade show environment. If you hit it off with a vendor, ask them to join you at the restaurant where you can talk business in a more intimate setting.

#8 Be Early

Try to get to the trade show as soon as it opens, especially on the first day. The best deals get bought up within minutes of the doors opening at most trade shows. The saying, "The early bird gets the worm," is accurate here.

#9 Work with Other Sellers

Most trade shows will have other Amazon sellers in attendance. There's strength in numbers here. You can oftentimes secure bigger discounts or exclusive deals when you combine your buying power with another (or several) other sellers. This lets vendors know that you're all serious. You may feel uncomfortable dealing with competitors but, trust me, there are enough great deals to go around.

Going to trade shows and following these steps can help you find a lot of new sellers to network with and companies to buy from. It's also great practice in negotiation, rapport building, and networking. The most important thing is to keep talking to the people you meet, even after the show is over. This will help you build strong relationships and do more business in the future. So, get ready, have fun at the trade shows you attend, and watch your business grow!

Finding and Utilizing Supplier Contact Information

Sourcing products to sell can be exciting, but the process often screeches to a halt when it's time to find supplier contact information. This can feel like a scavenger hunt, but don't worry! Let's cover some simple strategies you can use to find supplier contact information.

#1 Using Google

Google is your best friend when hunting for supplier information. If you're looking for a specific brand or distributor, just type their name into the search bar and hit enter. The contact information is often listed on their official website's contact page. But here's a tip: Don't just stick to the first page of the search results! Some suppliers are hidden gems located on pages two, five, or even beyond page 10. Spend some time digging through the results to find the contact information you need.

#2 Paid Tools

Sometimes, even a detailed Google search might not give you the results you want. Some suppliers have little to no online presence, making them harder to find. This is when paid tools come into play. One such tool is Seamless.AI. This is a huge data platform that supplies you with accurate contact information for companies of any kind. Although it's not cheap (around $140/month as of writing this book, and they lock you into a one-year commitment), the investment is worthwhile. Landing even a single solid account can offset the cost, paying for the tool for many years to come.

#3 Leveraging LinkedIn

Another incredibly underrated tool for finding supplier information for both companies and individuals at those companies is LinkedIn. LinkedIn is a goldmine for professional connections.

You can use it to find and contact the right people at brands and distributors. Just search the company name on LinkedIn, and you can find profiles of people who work there. Sending them a connection request with a note attached can get your foot in the door on a platform that very few wholesale sellers are using. A simple note I often include with a connection request goes something like this:

"Hi, we're looking to place a bulk order for brand name. Can you help?"

Short, sweet, and to the point. And it works.

#4 Go Beyond the Obvious

Remember, some companies operate under an entity that is different from the name of their brand, making them tricky to locate online. If you're having trouble finding a specific supplier, try searching for the names of their products instead. This can sometimes lead you to the official website or a contact linked to the supplier.

Compiling Supplier Contact Information

You've done it! You've found the contact information for the suppliers you want to reach out to. Now what? It's not about rushing to pick up the phone or shooting off an email. It's about being organized, patient, and strategic to make the most of the contact information you've gathered. Here's how you can use it effectively.

#1 Store the Contact Information Properly

First, make sure you keep the contact information in a place where you can easily find it again. You might be dealing with lots of suppliers, so staying organized is crucial. A customer relationship management tool, or CRM, is perfect for this. Our favorite CRM is HubSpot, and the good news is that it has a free version that works well for our business model. It allows you to neatly store all the contact information and keeps it handy for when you need it. You can create tasks within HubSpot to remind you to follow up as needed. If you prefer something simpler, a Google Sheet will work just fine. This way, you won't lose any valuable contact details and can reach out when you're ready.

#2 Don't Rush to Reach Out

Hold on before hitting that dial or send button! It's a good idea not to reach out to the companies just yet. Why? Because it's much more efficient to reach out to multiple companies all at once. This method is called batching, and it's a big time saver. Collect the contact information for five to 10 companies, and then set aside a specific time to contact them all in one go. This focused approach will make you more efficient and organized in your outreach.

#3 Create Email Templates

When it's time to contact suppliers, you don't have to start from scratch each time. Create templates. Draft a professional, clear, and concise email that you can customize for each supplier. HubSpot even lets you create templates and send the emails from within the platform. This step makes your outreach process faster and ensures you communicate effectively with each supplier. By using templates, you make sure your emails are consistent and contain all the necessary information, showing yourself in the best possible light.

If you want free email templates that actually work (the exact ones we used to land over 400 wholesale accounts), then scan the QR code below for a free download.

Building Great Relationships with Suppliers

Building lasting and positive relationships with your suppliers is essential for your Amazon wholesale business. Below is a guide, gathered from years of experience and conversations with suppliers, to help you become your supplier's favorite customer. It's a blend of things to do and things to avoid to create long-term and mutually beneficial partnerships.

#1 Pay Invoices Immediately

Timely payment is essential for a professional and respectful business relationship. Suppliers *hate* delays in invoice payments. Confirm the invoice details as soon as you can and pay them on time. This demonstrates your respect for their business and their time, and it shows you're a reliable buyer.

#2 Overcommunicate

A common complaint among suppliers about Amazon sellers is their lack of communication. Stand out by doing the opposite: overcommunicate. Be swift in responding to messages and returning calls. Clear and consistent communication about both what you're looking for and what you're not looking for helps suppliers to better cater to your needs, fostering a smooth and cooperative relationship.

#3 Provide Feedback

If a deal doesn't fit your business model, communicate this to your supplier. They appreciate this feedback as it helps them understand your preferences and expectations better. This openness paves the way for more tailored deals in the future, benefiting both parties. Don't go radio silent when they send you a bad deal. Let them know.

#4 Honor Your Orders

Please pay attention to this paragraph, as this is the most important thing you must do to maintain your credibility. Backing out of orders disrupts the supplier's inventory planning, straining your relationship with them. It kills your credibility and reliability in the business community. If you place an order, stand firm on it. This will keep them coming back to you with the best deals because they know you can close.

#5 Be Reasonable with Discount Requests

While negotiating for discounts is a standard business practice, please make sure your requests are reasonable. Excessive discount requests are disrespectful and will strain your relationship with the supplier. A polite no on a deal is more professional and maintains your integrity compared to a discount request that is entirely unreasonable.

#6 Send Thoughtful Gifts

A thoughtful gesture, particularly during the holiday season, will go a long way in the eyes of your suppliers. Sending gifts, or even a handwritten note, to your primary suppliers, is something that most people don't do. Because of this, the simple act of doing it is an easy way to stand out. They won't forget the gesture and they'll be that much more likely to want to work with you in the future.

Maintaining a healthy relationship with suppliers revolves around respect, communication, and professionalism. By promptly paying invoices, overcommunicating, providing feedback, honoring orders, being reasonable with discount requests, and expressing gratitude through gifts or notes, you set a solid foundation for a lasting and mutually beneficial partnership. This approach will easily set you up as one of the top (if not the top) customers. You may not be their biggest customer, but this will help you become their favorite.

Pillar #2 Contacting Suppliers

Dos and Don'ts of Contacting Suppliers

Now it's time to contact your list of potential suppliers. Here's what you need to know.

#1 Be Brief

When reaching out to suppliers, keep your messages concise. Suppliers are busy people, and they don't have time to read lengthy emails, especially from people they haven't met or done business with yet. Stick to a short, sweet introduction and a clear statement of what you're looking for. Your first email should simply and directly state who you are, what you do, and what you want. Extra information at this point can hurt you much more than it can help you.

#2 Be Specific About What You Want

Your requests should be as specific as possible. A generic inquiry is likely to be ignored. Suppliers prefer to deal with people who know exactly what they want, down to the brand, product, and quantity. Providing all these details, along with a target price, shows the supplier you are serious and well-organized.

#3 Respond Quickly

When a supplier responds to your initial outreach, provide any information they ask for as promptly as possible. A quick reply demonstrates your professionalism and commitment, showing the supplier that you are a serious buyer worth their time and attention.

Now, here are a few things you *shouldn't* do.

#4 Don't Mention Amazon Immediately

It's important not to mention Amazon in your initial outreach to suppliers. Most suppliers have reservations about working with Amazon sellers. I'm not saying you should lie about the fact that you sell on Amazon. Never do this. But if you mention it right off the bat, you're likely to get denied before you've even been able to get a foot in the door. Only bring it up later in the conversation, once the supplier can tell you're serious.

#5 Don't Overpromise

Be realistic in your initial discussions. Avoid making promises that you may not be able to keep, especially when it comes to the quantity of products you want to purchase. Setting appropriate expectations from the beginning helps to create a relationship built on trust.

Following Up Appropriately

Following up with suppliers is an art; it's the key to solidifying your supplier relationships. It's important to be persistent but not pushy. Here's how you can follow up appropriately and effectively, maximizing your chances of building a great partnership.

#1 The Three-Day Rule

A good rule of thumb is to follow up every three business days if you're not getting a response. Gauge the follow-up schedule based on the responses you receive. If the supplier responds with a hard no, it's usually best to respect their decision and move on. But if the timing isn't right for some reason, make a note of this and schedule a follow-up in a few weeks or months, depending on the conversation. Consistent follow-up shows your commitment and keeps you top of mind for future opportunities.

#2 Use Multiple Channels

If your emails are going unanswered, try other communication channels. Give them a call or send a text message. Different suppliers have different communication preferences, and some are more responsive on certain platforms than others. Varying your follow-up methods can increase your chances of getting a response and starting a dialogue. Just be sure to keep your communication professional and respectful, regardless of the platform.

#3 Contact Multiple Parties

If a specific person is not responding, try reaching out to someone else within the company. Use LinkedIn or the company website to find contact details for other relevant people. Different employees have different responsibilities and response times, and contacting multiple parties increases your chances of getting through to the right person.

#4 If Denied, Ask Permission to Follow Up Later

Rejection is not the end of the road. Some of the best accounts may say no initially. If you are told no, respectfully ask for permission to follow up after a set period. An example could be checking in once a quarter. Be faithful in following up as agreed. One of our best accounts was secured after three and a half years of quarterly follow-ups, proving the power of persistence and respectful, consistent communication.

Using these strategies shows suppliers your professionalism, seriousness, and respect for their time and business. Remember, each follow-up is an opportunity to demonstrate your commitment, value, and partnership potential. Approach it thoughtfully and respectfully, and you'll set the stage for successful, long-lasting supplier relationships.

Strategies for Contacting Suppliers: Combo Hits

Now let's dive deep into different strategies for contacting your suppliers. First, I want to tackle "combo hits," or the use of multiple channels, as I mentioned in the previous chapter.

Suppliers are contacted by many (sometimes hundreds) of Amazon sellers per week. It can be extremely difficult to break through the noise. This is where the combo hits strategy comes into play. It's called combo hits because it involves hitting a supplier with communication from multiple angles simultaneously, increasing the likelihood of getting a response.

Step #1 Start with an Email

Kick off by sending a concise, clear email to the supplier. Tell them who you are and what you're looking for. Mention specific brands and products you want to purchase. Even better, tell them the exact quantities as well as the price point that you want. This level of clarity positions you as a serious buyer. And suppliers love serious buyers. Use a straightforward email template, like the ones you can get for free by scanning the QR code in the previous chapter. An example could be:

> "Hi, we are looking to place a bulk order for Brand X. We have a list of SKUs and quantities ready. I just need to know who to send them to. Can you help?"

This direct approach outlines your request clearly, showing the supplier you mean business.

Step #2 Follow Up with LinkedIn

Almost immediately after sending the email, send a LinkedIn connection request to the relevant contact person at the supplier company. Attach a note summarizing your email, such as:

"Hi, I just sent you an email regarding a bulk order for Brand X. Can you help with this?"

This step reinforces your email and adds a personal touch, showing your initiative and interest in forming a partnership.

Step #3 Make a Call

A couple of hours after your email and LinkedIn message, make a phone call to the supplier. Inform them about the email you sent and express your readiness to place an order. Discuss the SKUs and quantities, showing your eagerness to put money in their pockets as quickly as possible.

"Hello, I sent you an email earlier regarding a bulk order for Brand X. We have a list of SKUs and quantities and are ready to proceed once we have pricing. Could you put me in touch with someone in sales so we can get this squared away?"

This three-pronged strategy substantially enhances the chance of getting a response from the supplier. Here's why.

- **Multiple Touchpoints:** Communicating via email, LinkedIn, and phone call covers various mediums, increasing visibility and showing you're serious.
- **Timeliness:** This strategy will get you more responses in less time, making it a more efficient way to do outreach.
- **Clarity and Consistency:** Sending your message across different platforms ensures that your request is clear and consistent, eliminating any confusion.

The combo hits strategy is an effective method of ensuring your communication does not get lost in the shuffle, helping you to stand out and receive more responses and faster. This tactic not only demonstrates your professionalism and determination; it also respects the supplier's time by presenting clear and consistent communication.

Strategies for Contacting Suppliers: Triple Dial

Suppliers are busy. Sometimes, in order to break through the noise, you need to think outside the box. The "triple dial" strategy is a game-changer, saving you time by getting you on the phone with suppliers fast. Simple in its approach but powerful in execution, the triple dial strategy involves calling a supplier three times in quick succession (if they do not answer the first or second time).

Here's how to execute this approach.

1) First Call

Dial the supplier's number. Wait for the ring. If there's no answer, hang up.

2) Second Call

Immediately call back. No answer? It's time for the third call.

3) Third Call

Dial the supplier once again, without delay.

This rapid-fire calling strategy will get you a response on the third dial 80% of the time. People simply don't answer the phone for numbers they don't recognize. By the third call, the receiver knows they better pick up the phone, and when they do, you'll be presenting them with an opportunity to make money (i.e., you buying inventory from them).

Here's why the triple dial strategy is so great.

1) Increased Chance of Contact

The triple dial strategy significantly boosts the probability of getting in touch with the supplier.

2) Efficiency and Time Management

It saves time and effort by ensuring that your calls have the best chance of being answered quickly.

3) Demonstrates Serious Intent

This strategy shows your serious intent to discuss business, sending a clear message to the supplier about your priorities.

You might initially hesitate, thinking this approach may be too intrusive or annoying. However, the feedback and response to this strategy has been overwhelmingly positive. Suppliers typically engage in a normal conversation, rarely showing signs of irritation or annoyance.

In executing this strategy, it's crucial to maintain professionalism. If the supplier does not answer the third call, I typically won't leave a voicemail. I'll wait a few days and try it again.

The triple dial strategy is a powerful tool for getting you on the phone with suppliers who may otherwise ignore you. By giving you a higher chance of quickly connecting with suppliers, it sets the stage for productive discussions, helping you get down to business faster.

Positioning Yourself Effectively When Contacting Suppliers

Positioning yourself effectively when contacting suppliers is pivotal in establishing lasting relationships. This section dives into how to represent yourself, whether you're reaching out to distributors and wholesalers or directly connecting with brands.

#1 The Cardinal Rule: Avoid the "Amazon Seller" Label

As I said earlier, suppliers hate Amazon sellers. Simple as that. This is mainly due to past experiences and stereotypes about them being challenging to work with or too demanding. So, the first piece of advice: Never introduce or label yourself as an "Amazon seller" when reaching out.

Instead, focus on being a serious buyer:

- Highlight your intent to place significant orders.
- Demonstrate your knowledge about their product range.
- Articulate the potential for a mutually beneficial relationship.

You're more than an Amazon seller, and it's your job to convince them of that.

#2 Confidence Is Key

Embarking upon conversations with suppliers requires a good dose of confidence. This should primarily come from knowledge and doing a little bit of research in advance.

Start by knowing what you want.

If you're contacting a distributor, research and understand some of the brands they carry. If reaching out to a brand directly, be aware of their best-selling products and those for which you want quotes.

Here's what an informed inquiry looks like.

> *"I am looking to place a bulk order for [specific brand/product]. We think we can do considerable monthly volume here. Can we discuss pricing for a purchase of X quantity?"*

#3 Leverage Your Experience and Relationships

For experienced sellers, the associations and histories you have with other brands or distributors can be a compelling selling point.

Mentioning that you work with their competitors or carry brands they sell can make your proposition stronger and demonstrate your credibility.

For example:

> *"We've partnered with [Competitor Name] and have been distributing [Brand Name] across various platforms. I see similar potential with [Supplier's Brand/Product] and we're open to discussing further."*

#4 Navigating the Landscape as a New Seller

Being a newcomer doesn't automatically mean you're in a weak position compared to more experienced peers. Your research and connections can pave the way for a strong impression.

Ensure that your approach demonstrates your product knowledge and market awareness, emphasizing your potential as a reliable buyer.

Also, consider utilizing your network to increase your strength. Leverage your connections with other sellers to formulate a "buying group," pooling resources to facilitate bulk purchases.

#5 Strong Positioning: A Golden Rule for All

Remember: Positioning is not just about your current state but how you convey your potential and reliability to the supplier.

Even new sellers can position themselves strongly. Be sure that your approach communicates potential, reliability, and thorough research about the brands they carry (if they're a distributor) or about their best-selling products (if they're the brand).

Even if you have a track record, showing this level of effort with a well-positioned approach is crucial to avoid complacency and ensure ongoing success.

Reaching Decision-Makers

Getting to the core of successful negotiation and partnerships with suppliers involves interacting with the right people —the decision-makers. In the world of brands and distributors, your goal is to connect with those who have the power to say yes to your requests.

#1 The Importance of Connecting with Decision-Makers

Always aim high. Strive to speak with those who hold decision-making power, such as salespeople or owners, especially when contacting smaller brands or distributors.

Work hard to bypass the gatekeepers. Avoid spending excessive time building rapport with individuals who lack the authority to fill your requests.

#2 Strategies to Connect with Decision-Makers

Straightforward inquiries work. Often, simply asking to be connected with a sales representative or another authority figure is all it takes to route your communication effectively.

Perhaps you're interacting with a small brand where the owner is directly involved in sales and partnerships. Your approach might involve directly inquiring about the owner's availability or asking for the individual responsible for facilitating wholesale accounts. On the other hand, in larger companies or distributors, asking for the sales department or a person responsible for managing wholesale accounts will likely guide you toward a decision-maker.

Be sure to define your request clearly. When asking to speak with someone, be clear about your intent—whether it's to open a wholesale account, discuss terms, or discuss another topic.

An example inquiry might be:

> *"Hello, I'm interested in discussing bulk purchasing and establishing a wholesale account for [Brand/Product Name]. Could I please speak with someone in sales to explore this further?"*

#3 Invest Your Time Wisely

Ensure the bulk of your interactions occur directly with those who have the authority to grant your requests.

Also, be sure to validate their authority. Even after being redirected to a supposed decision-maker, casually ask if they have the power to approve wholesale accounts or similar requests.

Utilizing LinkedIn to Contact Suppliers

Ready to dive into another hot tip to boost your business? LinkedIn can become your secret weapon for finding and getting in touch with suppliers and brands.

#1 LinkedIn: Not Just for Job Seekers!

Did you know LinkedIn contains hidden treasure for sellers like us? It's not just a place for job hunting but a perfect spot to find out tons of information about companies and the big shots who work there.

Use LinkedIn to unearth names, job titles, and more about people at companies you want to buy from.

You don't have to post every day (unless you want to!). You can sneak around quietly, gathering useful bits of information without making a big splash. Many Amazon sellers with corporate jobs use their LinkedIn for work, and that's fine. But sellers who post about their business on LinkedIn will find they get many more opportunities than those who don't.

I've started posting on LinkedIn daily about my Amazon business and it has resulted in tons of opportunities and connections in a relatively short amount of time since no one else is doing it.

#2 Talking to the Big Cheese

Guess what, savvy sellers? Sliding into the LinkedIn messages of big decision-makers at brands and distributors might just be the game-changer you've been looking for. Almost no other sellers are trying this trick, so it's like having a backstage pass! That also means your message is going to stand out big time. By trying LinkedIn, you're likely to get their eyes on your message much faster than on email.

#3 A Sample Template

Now, how do we reach out on LinkedIn? It's super easy! Send them a connection request and attach a succinct note like this:

> "Hi, I'm looking to place a bulk order for Product X. Can you help me out?"

Simple and straight to the point!

Email Outreach: Sample Templates

Talking to suppliers doesn't have to be complex! Here are some easy-to-use email templates, keeping the language simple and straightforward, that are ideal for striking up initial conversations with distributors and brands.

Template 1: Reaching out to Distributors

Subject: Bulk Order for Brand X

Hi,

We're looking to place a bulk order for Brand X. In particular, products X, Y, Z.

Could you put me in touch with someone in sales?

[Your Full Name]

[Your Company Name]

Template 2: Asking Distributors for a Quote

Subject: Quote Request for Brand X Products

Hi,

We're looking to get a quote on a few Brand X products. I have a list of the products as well as desired quantities, I just need to know who to send them to.

Can you help?

[Your Full Name]

[Your Company Name]

Template 3: Expressing Interest in a Brand's Products

Subject: Bulk Order - Product X

Hi,

My name is [Your Name] and I run a retail business called [Your Business Name]. We're interested in carrying your "[Name of Best-Selling Products]" and would like a quote on X units.

Are you the right person to contact?

[Your Full Name]

[Your Company Name]

Template 4: Initiating Purchase Discussions with Brands

Subject: Bulk Order for [Product Name]

Hi,

We're looking to place a bulk order for "[Product Name]." We're interested in a few more of your products but figured we'd start here as I know that's your bestseller.

Can you connect me with someone in sales?

[Your Full Name]

[Your Company Name]

When it comes to your outreach emails, remember your messages should be simple and straight to the point.

Feel free to modify these templates according to specific details of your transaction, ensuring that they remain clear and relevant to the recipient.

Also, if you want copies of these templates to use in your business (plus a few more bonus templates), scan the QR code below:

Pillar #3 Sourcing Products

Opening Supplier Accounts and Accessing Pricing

The backbone of your Amazon wholesale business is the products you source. Making sure you're consistently finding and buying profitable inventory is the key to sustainable growth. In this chapter, we're going to dive into the best methods for sourcing profitable inventory in a consistently effective manner. Here's an outline of what you'll need to have before you sit down and begin sourcing.

Step #1: Get the Product Details

Once your supplier account is open, you'll get access to product prices and details, usually via their website or a spreadsheet. This is your key resource for figuring out what products you might want to buy and sell.

Be sure to keep this information safe and easy to find for future use.

Step #2: Make a Brand List

If you're working with a distributor, create a list of all the brands they have. This isn't just a handy reference; it will also be useful for a sourcing strategy called the reverse sourcing method, which we'll explore later.

Keep your list easy to skim through—perhaps arrange it alphabetically or sort it by brand name.

Step #3: Use a Product Analysis Tool

Having a good product analysis tool, like SellerAmp, helps you quickly figure out which products might bring in good profits. This tool should help you make smart choices about what to buy without getting bogged down in too many details.

And there you have it—three straightforward steps to begin your sourcing process for your Amazon wholesale business. The journey ahead involves evaluating product choices and making smart buying decisions, which we'll explore in coming chapters!

Using UPC Scanners to Simplify Sourcing

Sourcing products for your Amazon wholesale business can sometimes mean sifting through hefty product lists from suppliers. UPC scanners have emerged as a powerful tool to expedite this, automating the finding of potential products on Amazon using the Universal Product Codes (UPCs) provided by suppliers.

Here's a step-by-step guide for using UPC scanners.

Step #1 Choose a UPC Scanner

Begin by selecting a UPC scanner. For instance, ScanUnlimited is a popular choice due to its swift, accurate scanning and competitive pricing.

Step #2 Prepare Your Price List

Ensure your price list contains the relevant UPC codes and is formatted and ready in an Excel or CSV file.

Step #3 Upload Your List

Navigate to your chosen scanning tool and upload your prepared spreadsheet or CSV file.

Step #4: Consider Search Filters

While UPC scanners will offer various filters to narrow down your scan, I recommend starting with minimal filters. Sometimes, applying strict filters may accidentally omit potentially profitable products.

Step #5 Commence Your Scan

Activate the scan and let the tool do its thing. Sit back and relax while your scanning tool automatically scans thousands (or even tens of thousands) of products in a matter of minutes.

Step #6 Examine the Results

When the scan is done, navigate through the results, ideally sorting them by sales rank. Evaluate each, and make sure they meet the three criteria mentioned in previous sections:

- Sold by Amazon less than 50% of the last year.
- At least two or three FBA sellers.
- Selling a minimum of 100 units monthly, or enough to be worthwhile.

Step #7 Highlight or Export Successful Finds

Finally, either star your winning products within the scanning tool or export them to a Google Sheet for later review and reference when putting together your purchase order (PO).

Utilizing a UPC scanner like this allows you to streamline the sourcing process, focusing your attention only on products that genuinely have potential and significantly cutting down your manual research time.

Reverse Sourcing

Reverse sourcing is like a treasure hunt on Amazon where we seek out profitable products to sell that we can source from our distributors or straight from the manufacturer. Let's learn how to do it step-by-step! But first, make sure you have these tools ready:

- DS Amazon Quick View: A free tool for Chrome that helps you see product details quickly on the Amazon search page.
- SellerAmp: A tool that helps you figure out if you can make money from a product.
- Keepa: A Chrome extension that shows vital product data.

Here's a simple guide for reverse sourcing effectively.

Step #1: Have Your List Ready

Start with a list of products from your supplier. This could be on their website or a spreadsheet they send you. This is where having a list of brands (if buying from a distributor) becomes extremely helpful.

Step #2: Search on Amazon

Pick a brand that your supplier carries and search for it on Amazon. Look for products that:

- are not sold by Amazon most of the time (less than half of the last year).
- have two or three other FBA sellers.
- sell at least 50 times each month or enough to make it worth selling.

Step #3 Check with Your Supplier

When you find a product that meets these three criteria, check your supplier's list or website. See if they carry it and, if they do, how much it costs.

Step #4 Use SellerAmp

Put the price into SellerAmp. SellerAmp will give you the estimated profit per unit based on your buy cost. Make sure your SellerAmp settings are correct, accounting for your cost to ship the product to Amazon and your prep cost (if you're using a prep center).

Step #5 Ask for "Special Orders"

If your supplier doesn't have the product but sells that brand, ask if they can get it for you. This is a "special order." This way, you might get to sell things that other sellers can't. These days, at least 30% of our orders are special orders. It's a huge competitive advantage that most sellers don't take advantage of.

Step #6 Make a List of the Best Products

When you find good products that can make money, write them down on a Google Sheet. When you're putting together your purchase order (PO), you can double check these products to make sure they're definitely winners.

Reverse sourcing is like being a detective. You look at Amazon, find great products, then check if you can also make money selling them. And sometimes, you can find special things that other sellers can't access if you ask your supplier to get it for you.

Using these easy steps, you can find great products to sell and make your Amazon business grow, month after month.

SmartScout Reverse Sourcing

Navigating through a supplier's huge product catalog, especially when they carry a lot of items from a single brand, can be a daunting task. Here, SmartScout steps in as a crucial tool for efficiently identifying the most lucrative products from a brand without you having to analyze each one individually.

Here's a step-by-step SmartScout sourcing walkthrough.

Keep in mind that this method works best when buying from distributors or directly from a brand that has a huge catalog.

Step #1 Have Your Brand List at the Ready

Begin with a list of all the brands your supplier carries.

Step #2 Navigate to SmartScout's Brands Tab

Go to the Brands section in SmartScout and utilize the Smart Filters to input a brand name from your list.

Step #3 Locate the Correct Brand and its Products

Select the correct brand from the result (watch out for duplicates!) by clicking the magnifying glass next to the name. Then choose 'Products' to view all of its associated products on Amazon.

Step #4 Implement Filters for Targeted Results

To zoom into potential products, apply filters such as: "A maximum sales rank of 300,000" or "An Amazon in-stock rate of no more than 50%."

Step #5 Ensure Products Meet Sourcing Criteria

Review the filtered results and open each promising product in a new tab, ensuring they meet your sourcing criteria:

- Less than 50% sold by Amazon in the last year.
- At least two to three FBA sellers.

- Selling at least 50 units monthly, or an amount that's worth your while.

Step #6 Verify Availability and Profitability with Suppliers

Check the product's availability on your supplier's website or catalog. If it's available, utilize SellerAmp to confirm its profitability by inputting the purchase cost. If unavailable, explore the possibility of special ordering it through your supplier.

SmartScout offers a systematic approach to identifying potential products from a specific brand on Amazon, easing the sourcing process by sidestepping the need to manually sift through each item. This tactic enables you to swiftly move from identifying potential products on Amazon to validating their profitability and availability through your supplier, ensuring a smoother and more efficient sourcing journey.

Unlocking More Inventory with Special Orders

Getting an advantage in the competitive Amazon selling space sometimes means thinking outside the regular inventory box. Special orders are a unique way to acquire specific products that a supplier might not ordinarily stock but can access due to their relationship with certain brands.

Here's a step-by-step guide to placing a special order.

Step #1 Identify Your Desired Product

Be precise about the product you want from a particular brand, even if your supplier doesn't usually carry it.

Step #2 Gather Necessary Product Information

Before reaching out to your supplier, arm yourself with this information:

- Product model number: Often referred to as an SKU (Stock Keeping Unit).
- Quantity: Define the number of units you intend to purchase.
- Target buy cost: Identify the price point you're aiming for per unit.

Step #3 Communicate Clearly with Your Supplier

Present this information to your supplier, telling them you're looking for a special order, and being as clear and transparent as possible.

Step #4 Wait for the Supplier to Communicate with the Manufacturer

At this point, the supplier will take your request to the manufacturer, discussing the possibility of acquiring the product in your desired quantity and at your target cost. Patience is crucial here, as it may take a few days for the supplier to hear back from the manufacturer and contact you with possibilities or alternatives.

Step #5 Evaluate and Decide

Upon receiving feedback from the supplier, look over the offered terms, and decide whether to proceed with the order.

Here are some reasons why special orders are a great strategy.

1) Unlocks New Inventory

Through special orders, you unlock access to products that aren't readily available in the supplier's regular inventory, potentially tapping into less competitive markets on Amazon.

2) Unveils Hidden Opportunities

This route often reveals products other sellers might overlook or deem inaccessible, giving you an edge in the marketplace.

3) Leverages the Supplier-Brand Relationship

Utilizing the established relationship between your supplier and the brand can allow you to quickly bring in products that may take much longer to source through other avenues.

4) Potential Profit Margins

By specifying your target buy cost, you can make sure it's a profitable transaction, if the supplier is able to agree to your price. You set yourself up for success from the beginning of the inquiry.

Be sure to use clear and transparent communication when going down the special orders route. Always be explicit with your supplier about your expectations and limitations.

Be aware that not all special order requests will be feasible. Be prepared for negotiations or alternate proposals from the supplier.

Also, don't hesitate to follow up with your supplier to keep the process moving and to stay updated on the progress of your special order.

How to Ask for a Discount

This is one of the most common questions I get from aspiring wholesale sellers: How do I effectively ask for (and get) discounts? Imagine you found a toy that was a big hit and you sold lots of it. Now you want to buy it again, but this time, you want it at a better price to profit even more from selling it. But how do we ask for a cheaper price without sounding pushy or rude? Let's look at some friendly and smart ways to tackle this.

#1 Order More, Pay Less?

Sometimes, if we buy more of something, we can ask if they'll give it to us for a bit less per item. This is often known as a bulk or quantity discount. So, we might say:

> *"Hey! That toy worked out really well for us last time. What if we buy X amount of units this time? What sort of price could you offer at that quantity?"*

#2 Let Them Choose

This one's easy. We let them tell us what we need to do to get a better price!

For example:

> *"How many units of that toy would we need to buy to get a quantity discount of some sort?"*

This puts the ball in their court. Sometimes, they'll come back with a better price than you expected.

#3 The Double Order Trick

This one's a bit clever! We're going to show them two options and let them decide. But remember, we have to be clear that these two orders are only drafts and not a promise to buy, as we're still in the negotiating stage!

We start as follows:

- Submit a draft of Order 1, with a regular amount of toys at the usual price.
- Submit a draft of Order 2, with a much higher quantity of toys and a hypothetical discount applied to the order (five-10% is typical).

Then, we chat with our supplier, showing them both options, and say:

> *"We're ready to move forward with Order 2 assuming you can meet the price on the order. Otherwise, we're ready to move forward with Order 1."*

You'd be surprised at how often this method works. They'll do whatever they can to meet your requested price on Order 2 since the order is essentially a guaranteed sale for them of a much larger quantity.

The Friendly Discount Chat

When we talk about discounts with suppliers, it's important to be nice, patient, and understanding. We should always make sure that we're showing them that we value our business relationship.

So, even while we try these ideas out, let's make sure we're polite, flexible, and honest. Say please, and make it clear your intention is to do long-term business with them. If they can't give the discount, it's okay. We must be understanding and remain friendly. Always maintain high standards by sharing accurate information and keeping your promises. If we do it right, we'll get a better price and keep a good friend on our supplier list.

Using a Simple Purchasing Criterion

Diving into the wholesale arena often requires sellers to conduct many different calculations and adhere to lots of criteria and so-called "golden rules" for selecting products. Whether it's strict sales rank thresholds or particular per-unit profit margins, the flood of variables we have to balance can sometimes hinder our decision-making more than help. Embracing a simplified, straightforward purchasing criterion will not only demystify the product selection process but also construct a more transparent path toward profitability.

Keep it simple. It makes so much sense to focus on a singular, comprehensible metric:

What is the expected monthly gross profit from this product?

The application of this metric strips away the complexity and ensures you are laser-focused on a specific financial target. You simply need to establish a monthly gross profit threshold for a product and if a potential product meets or exceeds it, you can consider it for purchasing.

Here's a step-by-step walk-through of this strategy.

Step #1 Establish Your Profit Threshold

Identify and establish your expected monthly gross profit threshold. This could be $400, $100, or $50 per month, depending on your business size and investment capacity.

Step #2 Use Uncomplicated Analysis

Forget various micro-factors like sales rank, number of competitive sellers, and other variables, and assess a product merely by its capability to meet or surpass your defined monthly gross profit threshold.

Step #3 Adhere to the Threshold

Stick closely to your sole criterion. If a product is expected to bring in less than your defined monthly gross profit, it is disregarded, even if it fulfils other criteria.

Step #4 Consistently Evaluate and Replenish

If a product, post-purchase, doesn't consistently meet the monthly gross profit threshold, it should not be replenished.

Consider a scenario where your profit threshold is set at $100 per month. You stumble upon a product that moves only two units monthly but yields a $50 profit per sale, and you're the only seller on the listing. It meets your criterion since two units x $50 profit/unit = $100, aligning with your established monthly threshold.

This method works for a few reasons.

- **Simplicity in Execution:** It reduces the need for constant analysis of multiple different factors, enabling faster, yet informed, decision-making.
- **Automated Consideration of Variables:** This method inherently accounts for various factors like sales velocity, competition, and per-unit profitability without individually calculating them.
- **Scalability and Flexibility:** It effortlessly scales with your business and can be adapted by adjusting the monthly gross profit threshold as your business grows and the market changes.
- **Risk Management:** By sticking to a pre-established threshold, it indirectly manages financial risk. This makes sure you're always buying products that meet your financial goals.
- **Time Efficiency:** It saves time otherwise spent on multi-factored calculations, freeing up resources to focus on other important aspects of your business.

A simplified purchasing criterion like the expected monthly gross profit keeps your sourcing simple and focused. You're not bogged down with multiple calculations. This will make your life much easier (and your business more profitable).

Determining Purchase Quantities

When we're running a wholesale business on Amazon, deciding how many units of a product to buy is a big deal. It's a balancing act—we want to have enough to sell but not so much that we have lots of stale inventory if things change. So, let's talk about a smart way to decide how many of each item to buy.

One key rule, especially for folks who are new to selling, is to "go wide before you go deep." This simply means testing multiple different products to get a feel for which ones will sell at a good volume and profit. That way, you can find out what works best without spending a lot of money on stuff that doesn't sell.

Step #1 Placing a Small First Order

A test order is when we buy just a small amount of a product at first; enough to sell for two to four weeks, to see how it does.

We can use the SellerAmp tool to help us guess how many we'll sell in a month. Just take the estimated monthly sales and divide that by the number of competitive sellers. A competitive seller is anyone priced within 2% of the Buy Box.

This way, we can check if something sells well before we take the plunge and invest more.

Step #2 Buying a Bigger Batch

If our test order sells well and makes a profit, then it's safe to buy a bit more! At this point, we should aim to buy enough inventory to have about 30-45 days worth of stock.

We stick to about a month's worth of product because prices on Amazon can bounce around, and we don't want to end up with too much of something if the price drops.

Even after you start buying more, keep a close eye on how well products sell. The market can change, and we want our buying habits to change with it so we can continue buying products that are profitable and stop buying products that no longer serve our business goals.

Choosing the right amount of product to buy can be tricky, but by starting small, testing, and then carefully buying more, we can work within safe parameters while scaling our wholesale business responsibly. This approach provides a safety net while we figure out what products do well and which ones don't.

The Right Approach to Purchase Orders

Sending a purchase order, or a PO for short, is a bit like making a shopping list for your supplier. It tells them *what* you want to buy, *how much* you want to buy, and where to send it. Let's dive into the smart way to make and send our POs so we look professional and our supplier knows exactly what we need.

Step #1 Make a Tidy List

When we make our PO, we have to be neat and include the proper details to avoid confusion. Here's what we need to make sure to put on it:

- **Supplier SKU:** This is a special code that the supplier uses to know exactly what product we want. It can be found on their website or price list.
- **Cost Per Unit:** How much one item costs.
- **Quantity:** How many we want to buy.
- **Total Cost:** How much the whole order will cost.
- **Billing Address:** Where the bill should be sent.
- **Shipping Address:** Where we want the items delivered.

Step #2 Use a Professional Template

Sure, it might be easy to just write all of this in an email, but using a special template for our PO makes us look much more professional. Adding things like your company logo and/or website to your PO goes that much further in establishing you as a professional seller. If you don't have a template, don't worry! You can use the same one we use for free by scanning the QR code at the end of this chapter.

Step #3 Save and Send as a PDF

Once our PO is ready and looks great, we'll save it as a PDF and send it to our supplier via email. Even if we can order on their website, saving a PDF of our PO is smart; in this way, we'll always have a record of what we ordered and when.

Step #4 Don't Forget to Follow Up!

After we send our PO, it's a good idea to check in with our supplier and make sure they got it. Sometimes they're busy and they might take a little while to reply since many of them are juggling multiple orders at a time from many different buyers. So, be kind, not too pushy, and just remind them about the order until it's on its way to you.

Sending a clear and neat purchase order helps everything run smoothly and makes sure we get exactly what we need from our suppliers. Remember, an organized and friendly approach goes a long way in forging good relationships and establishing yourself as a serious and committed buyer!

Pillar #4 Shipping and Logistics

Prep Center or Warehouse? Pros and Cons

As we dive deeper into the world of Amazon wholesale, a big decision you'll face is about where to store and handle your products before they get to Amazon. You have two choices: set up your own warehouse or partner with a prep center. Each method is viable, but one may be better suited to you than the other, depending on your preferences and where you are in your selling journey. Let's dive deeper into the benefits and drawbacks of each.

Your Own Warehouse

Here are the benefits of using your own warehouse.

1) More Savings as You Grow

One of the biggest benefits to having your own warehouse is the fact that your space is a fixed cost. This means that as you scale your business and continue to buy more inventory, the average cost to prep each product will go down. The bigger you grow, the more savings you'll see per item. It's like buying products in bulk—the more you buy, the cheaper each piece becomes!

2) Control Over Quality

With your own space, you can personally oversee the product checks. You'll know if each item is up to standard. It's like being the chef of your own kitchen; you get to ensure every dish is perfect before it goes out. This level of quality control is helpful for sellers who insist on having a hand in the sourcing and prep process to make sure products get to the customers in a professional manner.

Here are the drawbacks to having your own warehouse.

1) Managing Employees

Running a warehouse requires a team. And with a team comes the challenge of hiring, training, and sometimes dealing with people leaving. Plus, there are extra responsibilities, like managing insurance and benefits and handling day-to-day challenges. These are huge considerations to keep in mind if you take the warehouse route. Dealing with employees is not easy.

2) Long-Term Commitment

Securing a warehouse often means agreeing to a long-term lease. This commitment can be awkward if your needs change—if you outgrow the space or face unexpected business changes, for example. And if you decide, for some reason, to shut down your business, a warehouse lease can put you in a tough spot.

Using a Prep Center

Here are the pros and cons of using a prep center.

1) Expertise and Efficiency

Prep centers are experts in their field. They specialize in getting products ready for Amazon and getting them shipped out in a timely and efficient manner. By using a prep center, you tap into this expertise, allowing you to focus on sourcing profitable inventory and other core parts of your business. Using a prep center lets both parties focus on their core strengths.

2) Handing Over Control

Trust is key with prep centers. You're relying on them to meet deadlines and maintain quality. Sometimes, this might mean waiting a bit longer or not having things done exactly how you'd prefer. Loss of control is something many entrepreneurs struggle with. If you can get over this mental hurdle, you'll be in a better position long-term.

3) Variable Costs

With prep centers, the cost structure is set up so that you pay per item. As you scale your business by buying more products, your total costs rise. While you might get discounts for bigger volumes, you'll still see your overall bill go up as you scale. This is a key consideration if you're growing quickly. A prep center is a variable cost versus a warehouse which is mostly a fixed cost.

Choosing between a warehouse and a prep center depends on your business goals and personal preferences. If you value control and foresee the development of large-scale operations, having your own warehouse might be beneficial. But if you prioritize flexibility and want to lean on experts for this part of the process, a prep center could be your ally.

The journey of selling is filled with decisions. Whichever path you choose, ensure it aligns with your business vision and resources.

My Experience with Warehouses and Prep Centers

When you walk the path of entrepreneurship, every step is a lesson. I want to share a personal chapter from my selling journey: The tale of my own warehouse and my switch to a prep center.

The Warehouse Days

Picture this: Every morning, I'd wake up, sip my coffee, and brace myself for a 40-minute drive to my warehouse. The warehouse was tucked away in a quiet, rural area, far from the city that I lived in. It was in a smaller town that didn't have a lot going on. Sounds peaceful, right? Well, while the setting was serene, the reality of running it was far from it.

Hiring reliable help was a challenge. Given the location, finding quality employees who were willing to commute or lived nearby was like trying to find a needle in a haystack. But the difficulties didn't end there. Our warehouse lacked some key facilities like a forklift or a bay door for smooth loading and unloading. This meant every shipment came with its own set of extra charges and complications.

The combination of these hurdles made me reassess. Was this daily grind truly worth it?

Switching Gears to a Prep Center

When I transitioned to a prep center, it felt like breaking free from shackles. No more long commutes, no more hands-on product handling, no more on-site employee management. Instead, I channeled my energy into what I loved and did best: sourcing profitable inventory. With the added time it freed up, I even expanded my team by hiring virtual employees to shoulder the sourcing work.

Yes, my cost per unit rose when I started paying for the prep center's services. But the peace of mind and focus I regained felt invaluable. Not only did my business prosper, but my quality of life improved dramatically.

For me, the prep center proved to be a game-changer. It fitted seamlessly with my lifestyle choices and business vision. But remember, every seller's journey is unique. I've seen folks thrive with their own warehouses, optimizing every inch of their space, and loving the process.

And, on the other side, many are like me, embracing the benefits of leaving that side of the business to a prep center.

The key is understanding yourself and your goals. What works for one may not work for all. But every choice, if made thoughtfully, can lead you to success.

How to Choose the Right Warehouse

Stepping into the world of warehousing is like venturing into uncharted territory. While the prospect of having your own space may seem enticing, it comes with its own set of complexities. Before you open your warehouse for business and begin prepping your own products, here are some critical points you must consider.

#1 Loading Docks

The significance of a loading dock can't be stressed enough, especially when you're dealing with LTL (Less Than Truckload) or FTL (Full Truckload) shipments. If your warehouse doesn't have a dock, then trucks need a lift gate for pallet loading. Beware, though, as this can attract an additional cost; sometimes over $100 per shipment. This expense adds up significantly over time. If you don't have a loading dock, you can use a forklift. Make sure whoever operates the forklift has the proper certification. Forklifts require regular maintenance and cost thousands of dollars to purchase.

#2 Insurance

Your warehouse is an investment, and it needs protection. Besides the standard liability insurance, if you have a team, workers' compensation insurance is a must. And for those bustling times like Q4, consider adding a peak season endorsement to cover the spike in inventory. Always loop in your insurance agent to ensure full coverage.

#3 Waste Removal

Packing and unpacking can produce a surprising amount of waste. Before you know it, you'll be drowning in discarded wrapping and boxes. Factor in the costs of regular waste removal services to maintain a clutter-free warehouse.

#4 The Pallet Puzzle

Even though many shipments arrive on pallets, they aren't always in a usable condition. Having a reliable source for affordable and sturdy pallets is essential. Without them, your operations could come to a standstill.

#5 Warehouse Layout

Efficiency is the name of the game. The layout of your warehouse can significantly impact your operations. Regularly review and optimize the space to streamline your prep process.

#6 Payroll Practicalities

When you hire, you pay. And with that comes questions like how much, how often, and through what medium? Onboarding and offboarding employees also entails administrative challenges that you'll need to navigate smoothly.

#7 Handling Returns

Returns are a reality of retail. Designate a section of your warehouse for handling and processing returns. Create a robust system for evaluating, repurposing, or disposing of returned items.

#8 Sourcing Shipping Materials

Boxes, tape, bubble wrap, and more—they're all essential. Establish reliable vendors or bulk purchase arrangements to ensure you never run out.

In essence, a warehouse isn't just a large space to store products. It's a hub for numerous activities, and to make it functional, you need to think through every minute detail. While this book touches on some primary considerations, remember that the warehousing world is vast. Dive in with both enthusiasm and caution!

How to Choose the Right Prep Center

Choosing a prep center is akin to picking a strategic partner. When scaling your wholesale business, this decision can be a game-changer. The right prep center can streamline operations, enhancing efficiency, while a mismatch can kill your profit margins and impede growth. So, what should you look for when vetting a potential prep center? Here are some critical elements to consider.

#1 Seamless Communication

Above all, a prep center's ability to communicate is the most important factor to consider. You don't want to be in the dark about the state of your products or any disruptions in the supply chain. I am willing to pay a premium for a prep center that proactively communicates. Prep centers like these are rare.

A top-tier prep center will alert you in advance about potential issues, be it damages, shortages, or other challenges. This proactive approach allows you to troubleshoot in real-time, preventing larger problems down the line.

#2 Transparent Pricing

Hidden fees and convoluted pricing structures can rapidly eat into your profits. If your invoice is more than a few line items long, ask to get a simplified version.

Ensure that the prep center's pricing model is straightforward, with no hidden costs. As a best practice, obtain quotes from at least three different prep centers before you decide on one. This will provide a benchmark, helping you discern market rates and ensuring you're getting a fair deal.

#3 Advanced Technology Integration

In today's digital age, relying solely on manual processes or basic tools like Google Sheets won't cut it, especially as your business grows. Experienced prep centers with large clients will invest in advanced technology platforms tailored for order processing, inventory management, and real-time tracking. Having a robust portal like this will allow them to keep a close eye on your inventory and orders, ensuring precision and minimizing errors. Make sure they have the right tech to fuel a seamless operation.

#4 Prompt Turnaround Time

Time is money in the world of wholesale. The quicker your products move from the prep center to their destination, the better.

Before finalizing your partnership, have a clear contract in place. This should stipulate the agreed-upon turnaround times, ensuring there are no regular delays. Consistently missing these timelines can be a red flag and might warrant reconsideration of your choice of prep center. Great prep centers have an SLA (service level agreement) built into their contract. This means they're contractually bound to get your shipments out in the time frame specified in the contract.

The choice of a prep center can significantly influence the success of your wholesale business. The right one can help you to grow exponentially, whereas the wrong one will hold you back. Prioritize clear communication, transparent pricing, technological prowess, and prompt turnaround times when making your selection.

When to Start Using a Prep Center or Warehouse

Imagine this: Your bedroom is brimming with boxes, and your garage resembles a mini-Amazon warehouse. You know you're onto something big, and it's time to take that next step. You now need to decide whether it's time to get your own warehouse or outsource to a prep center. Let's discuss at which point it makes sense to go either direction.

#1 Outgrowing Home Operations

We've all heard stories of businesses starting from a garage (hello, Apple and Amazon). But there's always a tipping point. When products are spilling out of every corner of your house, it's time to consider more space. Whether you're crammed for room or you simply can't dedicate more personal hours to handling the business, a change is necessary.

#2 When to Go Down the Prep Center Path

Prep centers are a fabulous option when your shipping volume starts ramping up. If you decide you'd rather outsource to a prep center as opposed to getting your own warehouse, then pay attention to this section. The golden number? If you're consistently shipping over 500 units a month to Amazon, that is the point at which you should hire a prep center. At this point, you should be familiar with the nuances of shipping, making it easier for you to guide a third party on your expectations. A prep center is especially beneficial for those who want to focus on sourcing and scaling, without the nitty-gritty of packaging and dispatching.

#3 When to Venture into a Warehouse

Warehousing isn't a decision to be made on a whim. Opt for it only when it's the last resort, such as when your current space is bursting at the seams. A warehouse does come with its overheads, so ensure there's enough regular inventory turnover to justify its costs. Remember, while space is crucial, so is the financial prudence of not biting off more than you can chew.

#4 Think of Future Growth

When considering your first warehouse, aim for a Goldilocks situation: not too big, not too small, but just right. You should find a place slightly roomier than your current needs. This ensures that, as your business grows, you won't find yourself boxed in (pun intended) too soon. Avoid jumping into vast spaces too quickly, but do give yourself some wiggle room.

In conclusion, the decision on when to take the step from home operations to a warehouse or a prep center depends heavily on your business scale, goals, and personal preferences. Don't take the leap too soon if your business can't absorb the costs. But don't wait too long if your growth is becoming hampered by the limits of running it from home.

Shipping Options: SPD Versus LTL/FTL

Shipping to Amazon FBA involves juggling various factors, from product dimensions and package weights to departure and destination points. As the business scales, so does the complexity of shipping. Therefore, understanding the differences between Small Parcel Delivery (SPD), Less Than Truckload (LTL), and Full Truckload (FTL) becomes crucial.

#1 Small Parcel Delivery (SPD)

SPD is suitable for smaller shipments that do not require the bulk of an entire truck.

Carrier: If you're using Amazon's partnered program, UPS is the go-to carrier for SPD. Simply create a shipment in Seller Central and print the UPS shipping labels. You'll also print out individual box labels that you'll place on each box in the shipment. These labels tell Amazon what's in each box.

Package Regulations: Each box cannot surpass 50 lb and must stay under 25" on any side.

Ideal For: Shipments weighing less than 150 lb in total. SPD simplifies the shipping process for smaller sellers or those with lighter shipments.

Cost: Amazon's partnered rates make SPD a highly cost-effective method for such sizes.

#2 Less Than Truckload (LTL)

LTL is for larger shipments that occupy part of a truck's space but don't require the entire vehicle.

Carrier: While Amazon offers LTL shipping via its Partnered Carrier Program, you can also book with third-party carriers.

Package and Pallet Regulations: The rules for individual boxes mirror SPD—they shouldn't exceed 50 lb or 25" on any side. Pallets used must be 48" x 40", cannot tower over 72", and must stay below 1,500 lb. Ensure that every pallet side has a label, meaning there will be four labels per pallet.

Ideal For: Shipments ranging between 150 lb and 15,000 lb and encompassing up to 10 pallets.

Cost: Amazon's partnered rates for LTL are competitive, making it an economical choice for medium-sized shipments.

#3 Full Truckload (FTL)

FTL shipments use the entirety of the truck's space, either due to the shipment's size or the expedited need.

Carrier: Amazon doesn't include FTL in its partnered program. You'll need to contact third-party carriers or freight brokers directly.

Pallet Regulations: The stipulations for FTL pallets are the same as for LTL.

Ideal For: Shipments involving 10 or more pallets, and typically up to 24-26 pallets. However, anything beyond 10 could be more economical via FTL.

Cost: FTL offers the best value per pound when shipping to FBA. So, for large shipments, this is the best route to take.

Selecting the right shipping mode is a blend of understanding shipment size, costs, and logistic nuances. Aim to gradually shift toward FTL, as most seasoned sellers capitalize on its cost benefits. Efficient shipping is not just about transporting goods but doing so smartly, economically, and effectively.

Encouraging Suppliers to Ship Directly to FBA

One game-changing approach that streamlines the e-commerce supply chain is having your suppliers ship inventory directly to Amazon's fulfillment centers. This eliminates the need for an intermediary (like a prep center), saves on associated costs, and gets products to market much quicker. Here's how you can persuade your suppliers to ship to Amazon on your behalf.

#1 Exploring Suppliers with Existing FBA Prep Services

A growing number of suppliers now offer FBA prep services. They've recognized the increasing reliance sellers have on Amazon and have adjusted their offerings to cater to this demand. Many times, these suppliers can offer better prep rates than even Amazon. If your supplier provides this, the process is straightforward: Simply ask them to include prep in their service package. They'll consolidate the costs, and you'll find yourself paying for both the products and the prep in a single invoice.

#2 Guiding Inexperienced Suppliers

Not all suppliers are acquainted with the intricacies of FBA prep. If they're inexperienced in this area, Amazon can be your savior. When setting up your shipment in Seller Central, simply select the option for Amazon to handle the prep. With this in place, approach your supplier with a simple request: "Would you be able to ship our orders if we supplied prepaid shipping labels and specific box labels for each package?" This can be a huge win-win for both you and your supplier, especially if they normally offer free shipping. When you offer to provide shipping labels, you remove the burden of paying for the shipping from your supplier, saving them money. Many times, they're more than happy to do this for you because of the cost benefit.

#3 Persistence and Relationship Building

Building rapport and trust with your suppliers is critical. Some suppliers may initially hesitate to ship directly to Amazon due to not being familiar with the process or thinking it may take more effort than it really does. However, as you consistently order from them and nurture the relationship, they're more likely to consider your request. A strong business relationship often opens doors to greater flexibility.

In essence, getting suppliers to ship directly to Amazon can be as simple as posing the question to your supplier. However, it's equally important to approach it strategically, underscoring the mutual benefits and offering solutions for any concerns they might have. Remember, a streamlined supply chain can hugely enhance efficiency and profitability when you are running an Amazon wholesale business.

Arranging LTL Shipments

Navigating the realm of Less Than Truckload (LTL) shipments can seem daunting at first, but by understanding your options and making informed decisions, you can ensure your products reach Amazon's fulfillment centers efficiently and cost-effectively. Here's a breakdown of how to arrange your LTL shipments.

#1 Using Amazon's Partnered Carrier Program

When it comes to affordability, Amazon's Partnered Carrier Program usually takes the crown. Due to the immense volume of shipments Amazon manages, they've negotiated highly competitive rates with their partnered carriers. By leveraging this program, you can enjoy substantial savings. However, there's a notable catch: time. LTL shipments under this program, while cost-effective, typically take longer to reach their destination compared to using third-party carriers.

#2 Exploring Freight Brokers

If speed is more of a priority, or if you're seeking alternative options, freight brokers can be a game-changer. Platforms like Unishippers and Freightquote, among others, play the role of intermediaries. You provide them with your shipment details, and they scout for the best quotes from a multitude of carriers. Upon presenting you with the various options, they'll take a nominal fee for facilitating the deal. The beauty of this approach is the convenience and the competitive pricing they can fetch due to their industry relationships.

#3 Direct Carrier Engagement

Want to go direct? Many carriers, recognizing the needs of today's businesses, have set up user-friendly web portals. Here, you can quickly input your shipment information, get an instant quote, and if it aligns with your budget, finalize the shipment details on the spot. The advantage is the direct communication and the potential for building a lasting relationship with the carrier for future shipments.

#4 Why Freight Brokers Might Be Your Best Bet

While the direct approach has its merits, we've found that using freight brokers often delivers the best balance of cost and service. Their industry connections, combined with their ability to negotiate and shop around, usually results in a more favorable rate for you, especially when compared to the standalone rates many businesses might receive directly from carriers.

The method you choose for your LTL shipments should reflect your priorities, be it cost, speed, or a balance of both. It's essential to be aware of the trade-offs and benefits each option presents, ensuring that your products not only arrive at Amazon's doors but do so in a manner that best supports your business model.

Arranging FTL Shipments with Amazon Freight

Full Truckload (FTL) shipments, as the name suggests, take up an entire truck's capacity and are intended for larger quantities of goods. Given the volume involved, ensuring a seamless shipping process is crucial. Here's what you need to know about arranging FTL shipments for Amazon.

#1 Navigating Amazon's Offerings

It's essential to note upfront that the Partnered Carrier Program, a popular choice for many Amazon sellers, does not cater to FTL shipments. This means that if you're aiming for an FTL shipment, you'll have to seek external carriers or dive into the world of Amazon Freight.

#2 Amazon Freight: The Game-Changer

Different from the Partnered Carrier Program, Amazon Freight is Amazon's independent freight wing. As of now, it stands out as one of the most cost-effective and swift options for FTL shipping for a few compelling reasons.

- **Live Unloading:** This is the standout feature of using Amazon Freight for FTL shipments. With live unloading, your inventory is checked in real time as it's offloaded from the truck. This eliminates the cumbersome waiting period, which often involves days or even weeks when using other shipment methods, before the inventory gets processed.
- **Ease of Booking:** The process is straightforward. Head over to https://freight.amazon.com, create a shipper account, and you're ready to set up your shipments. The platform's intuitive design ensures that even those new to FTL shipments can navigate it and book without a hassle.
- **Flexible Payment Terms:** Cash flow can be a concern, especially when dealing with significant shipment volumes. Amazon Freight alleviates this stress by offering Net 30 payment terms for new shippers. This essentially means you can settle your freight bill up to 30 days after the invoice date, providing valuable breathing space for your finances.

Opting for FTL shipments requires a deep understanding of your needs and the best ways to fulfill them. While there are multiple third-party carriers in the market, Amazon Freight's unique benefits, especially live unloading and favorable payment terms, make it an appealing choice for many sellers. Always ensure you're well-informed and make decisions that align with your business's scale and requirements.

Utilizing 2D Barcodes for Efficient Wholesale Prep

In the fast-paced world of Fulfillment by Amazon (FBA), efficiency is everything. As sellers scale their operations, every second saved in prep and shipping can have a substantial impact on profits and productivity. This is where 2D barcodes come into play, offering a modern solution to an age-old challenge. Let's delve into how they can revolutionize your FBA operations.

2D barcodes are great for several reasons.

#1 Enhanced Data Capacity

The distinguishing feature of 2D barcodes is their data capacity. Unlike the linear barcodes of the past, these advanced symbols can hold a wealth of information—from product specifics to expiration dates and serial numbers—all condensed into a compact square.

#2 Boosted Efficiency

By integrating vast amounts of data within a single barcode, you drastically reduce the need for FBA workers to juggle multiple data sources. A single scan can provide everything they need, expediting the processing and handling of shipments.

#3 Durability That Delivers

One of the inherent advantages of 2D barcodes is their resilience. Even if part of it becomes compromised—be it via smudging, tearing, or scratching—the encoded data can often be deciphered, ensuring no hiccups in the processing chain.

#4 Versatile Viewing

Say goodbye to those cumbersome moments of trying to align barcodes perfectly for scanning. 2D barcodes don't play hard to get; they can be interpreted from virtually any angle, streamlining the scanning process.

If you're nodding along but wondering how to jump onto the 2D barcode bandwagon, we have just the solution for you. Meet 2D Workflow, dedicated software crafted by Larry Lubarsky, an esteemed, eight-figure Amazon seller. Larry streamlined his operation using 2D barcodes, cutting out two full days from his weekly prep routine. This software brings that efficiency to you, making the creation and application of 2D barcodes utterly seamless.

2D barcodes are not just a fleeting trend; they are the future of efficient FBA operations. They promise not only savings in time but also a noticeable reduction in operational expenses. Interested in giving 2D Workflow a spin? Scan the QR code below and embark on your journey toward optimized FBA prepping and shipping.

Choosing a Credit Card for Shipping Expenses

In the world of Amazon wholesale, where operational costs are high and margins can be thin, every penny counts. But it's not just about finding the best shipping rates or the most efficient shipping method; it's also about optimizing the way you pay for these expenses. This is when you should consider using business credit cards, which, when chosen wisely, can turn your regular shipping expenses into rewards or cash back, effectively giving you a discount on every dollar spent.

Here are my top recommended credit cards for shipping costs.

#1 American Express Gold Card

Known for its flexibility, the Amex Gold offers tailored benefits that adjust based on where your business spends the most.

For example, every month, this card rewards you with four points for every dollar spent on your top two spending categories out of their provided list of six. Conveniently, one of these categories is US purchases for shipping. This means, if shipping is one of your major expenses, you could be raking in the points.

#2 Capital One Spark Cash for Business

For a simpler reward structure that offers straight cash back, this card might be your best bet.

With the Spark Cash card, what you see is what you get—a clean 2% cash back on every purchase, with no caps or categories to keep track of. Whether you're paying for shipping or buying office supplies, every expense earns you a consistent 2% back, simplifying your rewards and ensuring a steady return on your spending.

The best card for your shipping expenses really boils down to your preferences. If you love the thrill of maximizing points and potentially using them for travel or other rewards, the Amex Gold might be your card. However, if you appreciate a straightforward cash back system without the fuss of tracking categories, then Capital One Spark Cash for Business should be your go-to.

Exclusive Offer

Either of these card options can add huge value to your wholesale business. I use both of them in my business, daily. If you want to look into either of these options, scan the QR codes below. If you sign up using either of these codes, we'll both get bonus points!

Understanding Shipping Costs to Prevent Leakage

In the world of Amazon FBA, the devil is truly in the details. Small oversights can become costly errors over time, and understanding these nuances can be the difference between soaring profits and sinking losses. This is where the concept of "leakage" comes into play.

#1 The Importance of Pinpointing Shipping Costs

Shipping expenses often comprise a substantial chunk of an Amazon seller's monthly outflow.

An imprecise calculation in shipping costs could pivot your operations from being in the green to diving into the red. It's essential to scrutinize every decimal place because, in a wholesale business, at scale, even seemingly small differences can add up into significant amounts.

#2 Amazon's Oversights: Reimbursement Management

Amazon, with its colossal operations, can occasionally misplace your shipments.

While Amazon does, at times, recognize these misplacements and provides reimbursement, it's not always the case. Sellers often need to initiate these reimbursement processes themselves to recover what Amazon owes them. This is a manual process that can take a lot of time, especially if you send in a lot of shipments.

With a large wholesale business, you'd need to hire a full-time employee whose sole job it is to contact Amazon to get reimbursements on lost shipments. However, this isn't the only route.

Instead of investing in hiring and training a full-time employee, which would've cost a couple of thousand dollars and a lot of our time, we chose to rely on specialized services that recover the cost of lost shipments. These services only charge a fee when they successfully recover your funds from Amazon, so they don't make money unless you make money.

For those intrigued by the concept, check out the service we partnered with: Seller Investigators. They've successfully reclaimed over $103,000 for us this year alone. Their efficiency is impressive, and the best part is the risk-free nature of their service since they only take a percentage of what they recover.

Want to try them out and see how much Amazon owes you? Scan the QR code below. As a bonus, you'll receive your first $500 in reimbursements from them for free.

#3 Phantom Returns

There are also instances where customers receive refunds and then don't return the product. Again, these might seem like small losses individually, but they can lead to thousands (sometimes tens of thousands) of dollars in losses over time.

These overlooked costs, lost shipments, and untracked returns might not seem critical, but in a scaled business, they can amount to thousands every month. To bring it home, consider that it took a whole five months for us to recover a shipment that Amazon lost of ours worth $24,000. I don't say these things to scare you, just to be honest about the realities of selling on Amazon.

In essence, understanding and addressing "leakage" is not just good practice; it's essential for profitability. It's about safeguarding your margins, and ensuring you're not bleeding money from places you haven't even looked.

Pillar #5 Hiring Virtual Talent

Organizational Chart for a Seven-Figure Wholesale Business

"If you want to go fast, go alone, if you want to go far, go together."

African Proverb

You'll hear plenty of people tell you that you need a massive operation with a small army of virtual assistants (VAs) to run a successful wholesale business. I disagree. You only need to fill a few critical roles. And what makes this even more intriguing is the flexibility to have these roles fulfilled by overseas virtual assistants, making the model both effective and economical.

Every effective wholesale business needs a reliable organizational chart. This is how I manage my organization and how you should as well:

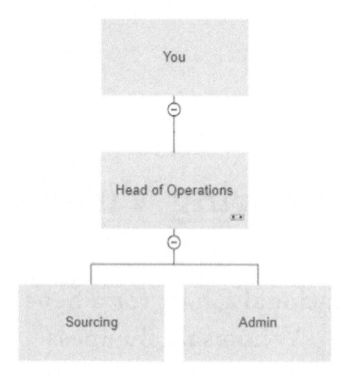

Here are the key roles in your business explained.

#1 You

These are the responsibilities that you really shouldn't delegate to an employee.

- **Closing New Accounts:** Your admin will bring you the account, but you'll see a much higher conversion rate if you take care of closing the deal.
- **High-Level Supplier Relations:** It will be your job to maintain a level of rapport with your suppliers, and only you can really do that.
- **Approving POs:** Always vet and approve any POs you receive. It's your business and your money.
- **Networking/Building Your Personal Brand:** You are the face of your company, and it will be your responsibility to maintain the personal brand and make valuable partnerships.

#2 Head of Operations

The HOO is your number two, and you must trust them with sales and team management. Their role is pivotal in ensuring that the business consistently maintains a profitable inventory.

- **Evaluating Leads:** A lead is only as good as its execution. The HOO critically analyzes leads provided by the sourcing team. They evaluate the potential profitability of each product, taking into account factors such as Amazon fees, shipping costs, market demand, competition, and more.
- **Draft POs:** Once the HOO deems a product promising, they draft a purchase order. However, before finalization, this order is typically sent to the business owner for approval.
- **Place Orders:** Once approved, it will be their responsibility to place the orders.
- **Day-to-Day Supplier Communications:** It will be their job to communicate with suppliers regularly and get back to you with any urgent information.
- **Manage/Train Team Members:** They will be responsible for managing and training the rest of the team.
- **New Supplier Research:** They will need to be actively and regularly looking for new suppliers, even if you aren't.
- **Submit RFQs:** They will be the ones to submit RFQs, so make sure they are trained to do so.

#3 Admin

Every business has tasks that, while not directly contributing to growth, are essential for smooth operations. The admin is the unsung hero who ensures that the backend runs seamlessly by dealing with tasks that, left unchecked, can accumulate and derail efficiency. They will essentially handle all the tasks that your HOO would otherwise waste time on. They will promptly answer emails, track down invoices, manage your sourcers and the administration of your seller account, and make selling decisions for you.

- **Manage Shipments:** They will manage the logistics and shipping of your inventory.
- **Seller Central Management:** Managing Seller Central is a relatively simple task that you can delegate to an entry level admin.
- **Repricer Management:** Managing your repricer is going to be a very important skill for your admin to learn to ensure everything is selling for the optimal profit.

- **Spreadsheet/Tool Management:** Spreadsheet literacy is one of the most important skills in today's economy, and your admin should be proficient in it.
- **New Supplier Outreach/Follow Up:** Managing outreach and follow ups helps you land new supplier relationships. A skilled admin can facilitate this.

#4 Sourcing

These will be the guys who are doing the trench work and finding new ASINs and brands to buy and sell.

The keystone of any wholesale business lies in sourcing profitable products. This role revolves around tirelessly scouring supplier catalogs and pricing portals, identifying potential leads on brands and products that promise good returns. After identifying these promising leads, the sourcing member sends them to the next important pillar of your business—the HOO.

When building a wholesale business, it's common for one individual, perhaps even the business owner, to juggle multiple roles. This approach might be sustainable in the early stages. However, as the business grows, specialization becomes crucial. Assigning individual roles to dedicated virtual assistants ensures that each function is optimized, enhancing overall efficiency and profitability.

In essence, scaling a seven-figure Amazon wholesale business doesn't require a sprawling team; it needs a focused and specialized trio of supporting roles, efficiently handling their designated tasks. And, with the globalized nature of today's world, leveraging the talents of overseas virtual assistants can make this journey both affordable and streamlined.

Hiring Your First Virtual Assistants

As your Amazon wholesale business flourishes, you might find yourself juggling more tasks than you anticipated. The idea of hiring a virtual assistant (VA) to relieve some of that burden might sound tempting. However, the decision isn't as straightforward as simply feeling overwhelmed and taking the plunge. You have to choose the right time, do it with care, and prepare well. Here's a guide to taking those first steps toward hiring a virtual assistant.

#1 Signs of Overwhelm

Wait until you start "dropping balls" in your business. If you're missing tasks, forgetting deadlines, or constantly feeling like there aren't enough hours in the day, it's an indication that an extra pair of hands could be beneficial.

#2 Start Small

Once you've determined the need for assistance, resist the urge to delegate large chunks of your operation immediately. Begin with simpler tasks. Let your VA manage emails, help with supplier applications, or oversee some aspects of your Seller Central. This initial period not only eases you into the world of virtual management but also helps you gauge the reliability and skills of your new VA.

#3 Keep Critical Tasks Close

It's a common pitfall to hand off essential tasks like sourcing products right off the bat. This strategy, although tempting, can backfire. Sourcing, being integral to your business's core, should be one of the last tasks you delegate. Familiarize your VA with the business's intricacies before trusting them with such a critical function.

#4 What to Outsource First

This is the order in which I would outsource specific roles, the top being the first thing I would outsource, and the bottom being the last.

Whenever you outsource, ask yourself, "What tasks can I outsource that don't 'move the needle'?"

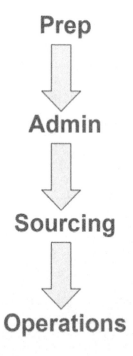

#5 Systems and SOPs Are Your Best Friends

The key to a harmonious working relationship with a VA lies in clarity. Before making that hire, ensure you have robust systems in place. Draft clear standard operating procedures (SOPs) for every task you intend to delegate. These SOPs will serve as a blueprint, guiding your VA step-by-step. It eliminates ambiguity and sets clear expectations. When onboarding, your primary role will be to train the VA on these SOPs, ensuring they understand and can execute them effectively.

In essence, hiring a virtual assistant is not just about freeing up your time; it's a strategic move to enhance productivity without compromising on quality. The key is to approach this decision with good preparation and a clear understanding of what tasks to delegate and when. Once this synergy is achieved, your VA can be a significant asset in your business's growth trajectory.

Key VA Performance Indicators to Monitor

The effectiveness of your virtual assistants (VAs) can often be quantified. By monitoring specific key performance indicators (KPIs), you can gauge how well each VA is performing in their designated role, ensuring your Amazon wholesale business operates at optimal efficiency. Here's a breakdown of the KPIs to consider for each role.

#1 Sourcing Team Member

The efficacy of your sourcing VA can be boiled down to their ability to identify profitable products. Here are the primary KPIs for this role:

- **Number of New Products Found:** This is a simple count of the new products the sourcing team member identifies. It gives an idea of their active searching capabilities.
- **Number of New Products Approved by the Buyer:** Not all products found will be viable. This metric sheds light on the relevance and quality of the sourced products.
- **Number of Products Replenished:** This metric focuses on the longevity and sustained profitability of the products sourced. If a product is continually reordered, it suggests that the sourcing VA's choices have a lasting positive impact on your inventory.

#2 Head of Operations

Your head of operations (HOO) is your buyer, and they play a crucial role in the profitability equation. Their decisions directly impact your bottom line. Here are their primary KPIs.

- **Total Spend:** This is the aggregate amount the buyer spends on inventory purchases. It helps monitor the budget and assess buying trends.
- **Weekly Gross Profit:** This is a measure of profitability after the cost of goods sold is subtracted from total revenue for the week. It's a clear indicator of the financial health of the purchases.
- **Weekly Gross Margin:** This percentage indicates the profit margin on the products bought. A higher gross margin suggests that your HOO is securing inventory at cost-effective rates.

#3 Admin

The role of an admin is multifaceted, and their KPIs can therefore be diverse, depending on the specifics of their responsibilities. A few notable KPIs include:

- **Number of Account Health Violations:** Keeping a tab on this ensures that the admin is effectively managing the seller account, maintaining its good standing.
- **Voice of the Customer Ratings:** By monitoring customer feedback, the admin can proactively identify and address issues, ensuring customer satisfaction.
- **Number of Shipments Picked up on Time:** Timely shipping is critical for getting products to Amazon quickly and optimizing cash flow. This KPI ensures logistical efficiency.

Each VA has a distinct role to play in your business's success. By setting clear KPIs, you not only measure their performance but also provide them with tangible goals to strive for. Regularly reviewing these metrics ensures that your business remains on track and your VAs are aligned with your overarching objectives.

Where to Find Virtual Assistants

Navigating the world of remote hiring can be daunting. With so many hiring platforms vying for attention, how do you find out where the cream of the virtual assistant crop resides? Let's break down the three leading platforms and discern which is most appropriate based on your specific needs.

#1 Upwork.com

Upwork is a renowned freelancer marketplace, housing an array of talent spanning across a range of fields. Here's what you need to know:

- **Specialty:** Upwork shines when you're in the market for specialized skills, particularly in the realms of development and technical expertise.
- **Broad Geographical Spread:** The platform boasts a diverse talent pool stemming from the Middle East, Eastern Europe, and Asia, offering a wide range of expertise and cultural backgrounds.
- **Pricing:** It's important to note that Upwork takes a sizable chunk of each freelancer's fees, translating to a higher cost for employers. However, the breadth and depth of talent available often justifies the premium.

#2 Onlinejobs.ph

Onlinejobs.ph holds a special place in the virtual hiring space, offering a niche focus on Filipino virtual assistants:

- **Specialty:** This platform is a goldmine for dedicated, long-term virtual employees. The Filipino work culture, which marries dedication with a keen understanding of Western business norms, makes this platform stand out.
- **In-Depth Hiring Process:** Unlike other platforms, Onlinejobs.ph requires a more hands-on approach. Employers post job listings, sift through applications, conduct interviews, and make hiring decisions. The responsibility of vetting and selection falls squarely on the employer.
- **Pricing:** One of Onlinejobs.ph's strong suits is its pricing model. While there's an initial cost to access the platform, you can terminate your membership post-hire, ensuring cost-effectiveness in the long run.

#3 Fiverr

Fiverr is a colossal freelance marketplace, known for its project-based model:

- **Specialty:** Fiverr excels at one-off projects. Whether you need a snazzy logo, a revamped website, or a brief research task, Fiverr's vast pool of freelancers can deliver.
- **Task-Based Model:** This platform is perfect for short-term gigs, but it might not be the ideal place to go if you're in the market for a long-term virtual employee.
- **Pricing:** Fiverr offers a wide range of pricing based on the expertise and ratings of the freelancers. It's easy to find both budget-friendly options and top-tier professionals.

Your choice of platform should hinge on your specific needs. Whether you're looking to complete a one-time project, seeking a specialized skillset, or you want a dedicated, long-term virtual assistant, there's a platform tailored to your requirements. We've used more than 50 different freelancers on Fiverr for various tasks over the years. We've hired more than 30 virtual employees from Onlinejobs.ph. We've also had special development projects completed by freelancers on Upwork. Each platform has its strengths and weaknesses.

Want to hire a VA but not sure what to put in the job description? Scan the QR code below to get free access to our VA job posting templates (the same ones I've used to hire more than 30 VAs).

Hiring Overseas Versus Domestic

Navigating the recruitment landscape for your business involves understanding the pros and cons of various hiring choices. In this era of global connectivity, businesses often face the decision of hiring virtual, often overseas employees, or sticking to traditional, US-based employees. Here's an in-depth look at the strengths and challenges of both options.

The Pros and Cons of Virtual Employees

Let's start with the pros.

1) Cost-Effective

One of the standout advantages of hiring virtual employees is the cost savings. While US-based employees could demand salaries upwards of $30,000, $40,000, or even $50,000 annually, virtual employees, especially those from countries with a lower cost of living, might only charge $6-10 an hour.

2) Cultural Compatibility

The Philippines, for instance, has a workforce that's in tune with US culture. Many Filipinos are employed by US firms, so they're often accustomed to American business etiquette and dynamics. This cultural understanding reduces potential friction and miscommunication.

And here are the drawbacks.

1) Training Challenges

Virtual settings can sometimes pose a challenge to hands-on training and quick feedback loops. The lack of face-to-face interaction may occasionally delay or hinder effective learning.

2) Decision-Making Hesitance

There's a stereotype (though not universally true) that some virtual employees might lean toward being "order takers" rather than "order getters." They might wait for clear directives rather than proactively making decisions.

3) Management Hurdles

Their lack of physical presence may sometimes make oversight challenging. Ensuring that tasks are being done promptly and correctly requires robust monitoring systems and trust.

The Pros and Cons of US-Based Employees

Here are the benefits of having US-based employees.

1) In-Person Training

Physical proximity allows for real-time feedback, in-person training sessions, and the ability to rectify mistakes immediately. This can expedite the learning curve and foster deeper understanding.

2) Immediate Availability

Domestic employees are often in the same time zone, which can facilitate easy communication and quicker response times.

Here are the downsides of US-based employees.

1) Higher Costs

One of the evident challenges of hiring domestically is the higher wage expectations, which can substantially increase overheads for businesses.

2) Limited Talent Pool

Restricting yourself to a specific region might limit the potential talent pool, especially when specialized skills are required.

The decision between virtual and US-based employees doesn't have a one-size-fits-all answer. It largely hinges on the specific needs of the business, the nature of the tasks, and the resources available.

In my experience, 95% of the tasks involved in a wholesale business can (and should) be handled by a low-cost, overseas employee, ideally from the Philippines. There are plenty of places to source talented folks such as onlinejobs.ph, Upwork, or Fiverr.

Strategies for Disqualifying Candidates

The quest to find the best virtual talent is like trying to find a needle in a haystack. With scores of applicants pouring in, the challenge lies not in attracting candidates but in searching through to find that diamond in the rough. Employing strategic disqualification methods can ensure that you identify top contenders swiftly and efficiently. Here's a guide to smartly navigating the vast sea of virtual job applicants.

#1 The Banana Trick: A Litmus Test for Detail Orientation

To make sure that your applicants read the job description entirely, use the banana trick. Somewhere in the job description, make a note that "to verify that you've read this job description, include the word 'banana' in your application."

It sounds trivial, but it serves as a clear barometer of an applicant's attention to detail. Surprisingly, a vast majority will overlook this, thus narrowing your selection pool to only the most meticulous candidates. In my experience, this can narrow the pool by about 80%.

#2 The Two-Pronged Attack: Speed and Eloquence

A reliable internet connection is critical for virtual roles. Requiring applicants to submit a screenshot of their internet speed test serves you two-fold: It assesses their connectivity and their adherence to instructions. Pair this with a request for a brief, 30-second voice sample, asking them to describe why they're suitable for the role, and you're not only gauging their English proficiency and clarity of voice but also their ability to articulate their value proposition in a concise manner.

#3 Batching Interviews: A Testament to Commitment

Scheduling interviews can be a huge pain for the business owner. Tools like Calendly simplify this process, allowing candidates to pick a slot. By restricting available slots to a narrow three-hour window, you're introducing another filtering layer. The candidates willing to shuffle their commitments around to accommodate this window demonstrate a higher drive and genuine interest in the role.

#4 The Trial Offer: A Litmus Test for Compatibility

The hiring process doesn't end with the interview. Extending a two-week trial period to potential candidates serves as the final vetting procedure. This not only gives you insights into their working style, skills, and adaptability but also offers the candidate a glimpse into your company's operations. By clearly communicating that either party can bow out if the fit doesn't feel right, it ensures transparency and reduces future complications.

In essence, the virtual hiring process isn't just about identifying skills; it's also about gauging a candidate's dedication, attention to detail, and commitment. By integrating these disqualification strategies, you're not merely shortening your hiring cycle but also enhancing the quality of your hires. In the vast world of virtual employment, they'll ensure that you're always a step ahead in securing the best talent.

Tips for Hiring Outstanding Virtual Assistants

Regular virtual assistants are a dime a dozen. Pinpointing the true gems in a crowded marketplace can feel impossible. However, with a few tricks up your sleeve, you can streamline this process and ensure that you're not only drawing the best candidates but are also set up for a harmonious and productive working relationship. Here are some key strategies to help you hire outstanding assistants.

#1 Asynchronous Interviews with Hireflix

Utilize platforms like Hireflix to revolutionize your interview process. Pre-record your questions and let applicants respond in their own time. It eliminates the logistical headaches of scheduling and lets you assess responses at your convenience.

#2 Gauge Their Current Commitments

Dig deep into their current job scenario. Most virtual assistants juggle multiple roles, and understanding this dynamic is crucial. If you're offering a full-time role, ensure they're willing to relinquish other commitments. This ensures your business gets their undivided attention, and there's no clash of priorities.

#3 Extract Relevance from Past Roles

Rather than just skimming through their CV, ask them how their past roles would benefit the current position you're hiring for. Their insights can reveal a lot about their analytical skills and their ability to adapt previous learnings to new situations.

Incorporating these tips into your hiring process will drastically increase your odds of securing a virtual assistant who isn't just competent but a perfect match for your business ethos and needs. Remember, in the realm of virtual hiring, it's not just about finding the right skillset; it's also about ensuring a harmonious synergy with the broader vision of your Amazon wholesale business.

Setting Expectations with Virtual Assistants

Establishing a successful collaboration with a virtual assistant isn't solely about hiring the right talent; it's equally about setting the right expectations from the outset. This ensures that both parties are aligned and moving in tandem toward mutual success. Here's how to effectively set the stage for a harmonious working relationship.

#1 Initiate with Onboarding Excellence

A strong beginning often dictates the trajectory of the working relationship. Before your VA's first official day, make sure you've completed the following:

- **Tech Setup:** Provide them with access to all necessary software, tools, and platforms they'll need for their role.
- **Payroll:** Walk them through the payment process, ensuring clarity on frequency, mode, and any related intricacies.
- **Timing:** Clearly define their working hours, factoring in time zones if applicable. Ensure both of you know when they're expected to be available.
- **Emergency Protocols:** Obtain an emergency contact number. This not only covers unforeseen events but also underlines your care for their wellbeing.
- **Communication Channels:** If they need an official email or any other communication medium, get it set up and guide them through the basics.
- **Essential SOPs:** Share the SOPs pertinent to their role to allow them a smooth start and reduce the initial learning curve.
- **Role Orientation:** Furnish them with any other specifics, be it cultural nuances of the company or small operational details, which will ensure they feel comfortable and informed.

#2 Set the Professional Tone

The efficiency of your onboarding process reflects your business's ethos. When VAs witness meticulous planning and attention to detail, they automatically understand the level of dedication and professionalism expected from them.

#3 Team Integration

Remember, your new VA isn't working in isolation. If you have an existing team, remember to introduce them and clarify how they will work with each other:

- **Introduction:** Facilitate introductions with other team members, allowing them to understand the broader team dynamics.
- **Role Clarity:** Clearly indicate the new VA's responsibilities vis-à-vis other team members. Such clarity minimizes potential conflicts and territory disputes.
- **Assuage Fears:** Address any latent fears among existing team members about the new hire replacing them. Reinforce that every hire aims to enhance the team's collective capabilities rather than make anyone redundant.

In essence, meticulous expectation setting is about eliminating ambiguities. By defining the lines clearly, you not only ensure operational efficiency but also pave the way for a relationship built on trust, clarity, and mutual respect. The right start can often be the difference between a transient work relationship and a long-term, symbiotic partnership.

Red Flags to Watch Out for During Hiring

Navigating the virtual hiring landscape can be tricky. While there's an abundance of talent available, it's essential to stay vigilant for potential pitfalls. Recognizing the red flags can help you filter out unsuitable candidates and streamline your hiring process to ensure optimal team dynamics and productivity. Here are some warning signs to watch out for:

#1 Lackluster Communication

The hallmark of a competent VA is robust communication. They proactively update you, seeking feedback and offering insights. A VA who remains elusive, evasive, or consistently late in responding is a liability. In the world of virtual assistance, silence isn't golden but a clear sign of potential issues ahead.

#2 Neglecting the Nitty-Gritty

Precision is the backbone of a VA's role. An assistant who overlooks details, especially in an intricate operation like an Amazon business, becomes a bottleneck. Minor errors, consistently repeated, or an inability to iron out mistakes, signals a lack of thoroughness, which can be detrimental in the long run.

#3 Conflict of Interest Conundrums

Protecting your business interests is paramount. For Amazon sellers, this is even more crucial. A VA involved with multiple FBA clients might unintentionally overlap tasks or share sensitive information. Ensure your VA's professional allegiances lie solely with you, eliminating potential conflicts and maintaining business confidentiality.

#4 Perpetual Pay Advances

While it's compassionate to consider occasional advance payments, it's prudent to be wary of regular requests. An agreed-upon payment structure is in place for a reason, ensuring clarity and trust. If a VA consistently nudges for advances, it may be indicative of financial instability or a lack of professionalism.

#5 Overstated Expertise

Resumes can sometimes be marketing brochures, highlighting the best while sidelining the rest. It's not uncommon for some VAs to magnify their skills during the hiring process. This is where a trial period is invaluable. If the VA struggles to match their claimed competencies within this period, it's a clear sign they might not be the right fit for your business.

While hiring virtual assistants can revolutionize your operations, it's vital to be discerning. Recognizing these red flags early can save time, resources, and potential headaches, ensuring your business continues to operate smoothly and efficiently.

Empowering Virtual Assistants to Craft SOPs

In the ever-changing world of business operations, standard operating procedures (SOPs) stand as crucial signposts. They ensure tasks are executed uniformly and optimally each time. When your workforce is dispersed across continents and time zones, SOPs become even more vital. What I've realized, over time, is that VAs are uniquely placed to create effective SOPs. Here's a guide to empowering your virtual assistants to generate these important business assets themselves.

#1 The Rationale for SOP Creation by VAs

Your virtual assistants, by the very nature of their roles, navigate a multitude of tasks daily. This places them in the unique position to document these processes meticulously. Getting VAs to create SOPs is not just about recording procedures but about building a knowledge base that's rooted in practical experience.

#2 The Observer-Executor Model

The essence of this model lies in having two virtual employees engage in SOP creation collaboratively.

- **Employee A (Executor):** This individual performs the task as they would on a regular basis. Their primary role is to be an example, focusing solely on accomplishing the task to the best of their ability.
- **Employee B (Observer):** As the name suggests, this individual is the silent spectator, keenly observing and jotting down an outline of the process as Employee A progresses. Since they are not well-versed in the task at hand, they'll take more detailed notes than Employee A would (Employee A may gloss over details because of how familiar they are with the task).

#3 Collaborative Review and Refinement

Once the task is completed, the duo converges to review the draft SOP. Employee A, with their hands-on experience, can validate the steps and provide clarification. They can elaborate on intricate details or nuances that might not have been evident to the observer. This dual perspective ensures the SOP is comprehensive and lacks any ambiguities.

#4 The Advantage of Cross-Training

Besides SOP creation, this method serves a dual purpose: cross-training. With Employee B now familiar with the task, you have a backup ready. It's a safeguard that ensures continuity if Employee A is unavailable.

Crafting SOPs through the observer-executor model capitalizes on the combined strengths of your virtual team. It ensures that procedures are not just recorded but understood in depth. Moreover, these SOPs, borne of collaboration, act as an invaluable resource, ensuring operational consistency and facilitating easier onboarding of future team members. SOPs thus become more than just documents; they become the bedrock of efficient virtual operations.

Lessons Learned from hiring Over 30 Virtual Assistants

After hiring numerous virtual assistants, I've gathered a treasure trove of insights that can help both newcomers and seasoned employers in the realm of virtual employment. Here's what I've learned from my experiences.

#1 Respect Knows No Borders

Geographical distance shouldn't create disparities in how employees are treated. Virtual assistants, whether based in the US or overseas, deserve the same respect and fair treatment. When you foster an environment of equity and appreciation, you cultivate commitment and loyalty in return.

#2 You Need to Earn Their Loyalty

There's a saying among seasoned VA employers: "Your VA is always working elsewhere; the question is where?" A fully engaged assistant is less likely to seek secondary employment. Ensure your VA has a full plate; an idle mind can wander, and so can their commitment. They're much more likely to remain loyal to you if you treat them well and foster an environment where they can grow and improve their skills.

#3 Mastery Through Repetition

Hiring virtual assistants isn't just about filling a position; it's a craft. The more you immerse yourself in the hiring process, the more adept you'll become at discovering that pearl in the vast sea of candidates. Experience hones your ability to discern potential rockstars from the rest.

#4 Patience, but Only Up to a Certain Point

While training a VA, patience is essential. However, you still need to strike a balance. If your VA struggles consistently despite having well-laid-out SOPs and diligent training sessions, it might be time to reassess their suitability for the role.

#5 Continuous Engagement Is Crucial

The misconception that VAs are a "hire-and-forget" solution can derail your working relationship. As your business evolves, your VA needs to stay aligned with its trajectory. Regular touchpoints, be it through Zoom, Slack, or WhatsApp, are essential to ensure they remain synchronized with your business vision and are held accountable.

My journey of hiring over 30 virtual assistants has been enlightening, filled with ups and downs. But with each hiring cycle, I've refined my approach, ensuring a smoother, more efficient process. These lessons, learned the hard way, are now yours to benefit from.

Getting Started

22-Day Action Plan

Embarking on the Amazon wholesale journey requires more than just knowledge—it requires decisive action. As the adage goes, "Knowledge without action is like a car without gas." Now that you're equipped with the essential information, it's time to use it. Here's a streamlined 22-day action plan to jumpstart your Amazon wholesale venture.

Day 1: Foundation Day

Today, lay the bedrock of your business.

- Establish your LLC.
- Open a business bank account.
- Obtain an EIN number—consider this the Social Security number for your business.
- Kick off your selling journey by opening an Amazon Seller account.

Days 2-8: Lead Mining Week

Dive into Pillar 1: Finding Suppliers.

- Aim to add five distributor leads and 10 brand leads every day. This will accumulate to produce a substantial list by the end of the week.

- Organize these leads systematically, either in a Google Sheet or in your preferred CRM tool.

Days 9-11: Initiate Contact

Now, leverage Pillar 2: Contacting Suppliers.

Using the handy supplier email templates provided (access them via the QR code in Pillar 2), get in touch with all the leads you've compiled.

Days 12-17: Persistence Pays

During this phase, consistency is crucial.

- Relentlessly follow up with leads that haven't responded every three business days.
- As applications from suppliers trickle in, prioritize them. Remember, swift action is key. Complete and return these applications within 24 hours.

Days 18-22: Product Analysis Phase

You're now stepping into Pillar 3: Sourcing Products.

As you start receiving product leads in various forms—be it from distributor price lists, brand catalogs, or websites—dedicate time to analyzing each of them methodically using the techniques you've learned in the previous chapters.

By rigorously implementing this plan, you're positioning yourself for success within the first 30 days. It's not merely a promise—it's a guarantee.

Want More?

Hungry for more nuanced guidance on your Amazon wholesale journey? For a comprehensive deep dive into starting, scaling, and managing your Amazon wholesale business, scan the QR code below. Check out *The Wholesale Challenge* and join more than 673 other successful wholesale sellers inside our exclusive community.

Diving into the Amazon Community on Social Media

Finally, I want to talk about the benefits of getting involved with the Amazon community. Selling on Amazon can feel like a lonely pursuit, especially when you're just getting started. I can attest to this. For the first five years of my Amazon journey, I could count on one hand the amount of other Amazon sellers I knew personally. However, once I began getting active on social media (on Twitter, in particular, now X) I began meeting other sellers just like me. My business grew much faster as a result. Joining social media is the very thing that led me to write the book you just read.

Why the Community Matters

The power of community in the Amazon selling world cannot be understated. A lone venture into the depths of Amazon wholesale can quickly become overwhelming. However, surrounded by a group of individuals who share the same aspirations and challenges, the journey becomes not just manageable but genuinely enjoyable. And the best part? There's an entire legion of such passionate Amazon sellers, who all congregate on social media.

Discover the Amazon Hub on Twitter/X

Where does this enthusiastic community primarily reside? The answer is Twitter/X. It's the bustling marketplace where Amazon sellers from various backgrounds and with varied experience share their insights, challenges, successes, and resources. If you're yet to make your foray into this space, I highly recommend setting up a Twitter/X account. It's not merely about following others; it's about immersing yourself in the community—engaging in conversations, seeking advice, and offering your own experiences.

A Warm Welcome Awaits

You might be wondering, "Will I be the new kid on the block? Will the community welcome a newcomer?" Absolutely! The Amazon community on Twitter/X is renowned for its welcoming nature. Most members are more than willing to guide novices, share resources, and answer questions. With such a supportive network, you're never truly alone on your Amazon journey.

Let's Connect!

Once you're on Twitter/X, don't forget to follow me: @GanimCorey. I'm eager to know your thoughts on the book and any questions or insights you might have about the world of Amazon selling. Slide into my DMs; I make it a point to respond to as many messages as I can and assist in whatever way possible.

Remember, every great journey begins with a single step, or in this digital age—a single click. So, dive in, start connecting, and let the incredible Amazon community be your guiding star.

Thank You

A quick note of thanks is in order for everyone that made this book a possibility.

First and foremost, my partners Christopher Grant and Nate McCAllister were instrumental in getting this book published. Before I met them, the thought of writing a book never crossed my mind. They pushed me to make it a reality, and I'm eternally grateful. It was a team effort.

To my family and friends (and my dog George!), thank you for all of your support along the way. It is truly appreciated.

And to everyone who has taken part in *The Wholesale Challenge,* thank you for making our community of 600+ wholesale sellers a welcoming place where people of all skill levels can learn the art of Amazon wholesale.

I look forward to hearing your thoughts about the book. I'm open to constructive criticism and positive feedback alike, so feel free to send your comments to me personally at corey@coreyganim.com.

Best of luck in your Amazon wholesale journey,

Corey Ganim

Printed in Great Britain
by Amazon